EMILY CAVE

For Colb

The Vow Beyond "Till Death Do Us Part"

Publishing Assistance by
B&T Publishing Services
Knoxville, TN • Nashville, TN

First printing, April 2023

Library of Congress Cataloging-In-Publication Data
Cave, Emily
    For Colb: The Vow Beyond "Till Death Do Us Part"
Emily Cave—1st ed.
    p. cm.
Includes bibliographical references.
ISBN: 9798397310239
    1. Biography 2. Inspiration 3. Sports 4. Hockey

Cover Design by Emily Cave
Cover Photo by Mango Studios
Author Photo by Emilie Iggiotti
Interior Layout by Tim Marshall
Printed in China

EMILY CAVE

For Colb

The Vow Beyond "Till Death Do Us Part"

"Colb, there are not enough pages in this book, nor words I could ever say to describe how much I miss you. Thank you for being the best sweet angel hubby. I'll see you in Heaven, hold it down 'til I get there. Agape."

Contents

Prologue

Tuesday, April 7th, 2020. The day that would forever change my life. It was the day Colby would undergo emergency brain surgery. We didn't know what the outcome would be. We had no idea if he'd make it through it. All we could do was wait. And wait. And wait. During that waiting game, I made a vow, to him, to myself, and to anyone that would be willing to listen, that no matter the outcome, I would do all that I could to continue to honor him by sharing his story.

Our story.

The story of us.

I have often thought about this moment — writing the first sentence of my book. I always knew that if I didn't use my pain and heartbreak to help others, I wouldn't be the woman Colby married. He nicknamed me his "little world changer." I don't know if I can live up to that name. That's a lot of pressure. But I do know that no matter how hard and scary it has been for me to be vulnerable about my grief, the thought of not living up to the vow I made that day, scares me so much more. That vow and our love for one another have been my motivation every day and will continue to be until we are reunited in Heaven.

Grieving is really hard. There isn't a blueprint for the perfect way to do it. I wish there was. It would make it a lot easier. But there isn't. In the days after Colby passed away, I felt like a shell of myself. I was a 26-year-old, who had just lost the love of my life and had no idea how to do life without him. I just did whatever it took each day to put on a brave face for our friends, my family, the media, and the millions of people that were watching my every move under a microscope. As I said, grieving is hard. Grieving while the whole world is watching, nitpicking at every post, every comment, every interview, and every move that I'd make, has been even harder to do than I ever could have imagined.

I remember thinking if I can just get through the next milestone, maybe I will feel a little bit better. My birthday. Our first wedding anniversary. The Colby Cave nights. Christmas. Colby loved Christmas. And he loved watching me love Christmas. His birthday, the day after Christmas. The memorial service at the one-year mark of his passing. The list could go on. But it's funny how with each milestone, another one was right around the corner. And to this day, they still haven't stopped. When you plan to do the rest of your life with someone, there will always be "firsts" that they should have been here for. Until they are not.

I can't pinpoint the exact moment, but one day it hit me, and I remember coming to the realization that I will never feel like I'm 'through this.' And that's okay. Because maybe getting through this, isn't the goal. Maybe it's growing through this. Maybe it's continuing to live through this. Maybe it's sharing and impacting through this. Colb's life mattered. The way he lived. The way he loved. It all mattered. And as I'm writing these words, with tears streaming down my face, I can almost see him up there, with a front-row seat, cheering me on like crazy, just like I used to cheer him on at his hockey games. I bet he's even up there telling all his buddies, "That's my little world changer. Look at her go." Just like I'd tell my friends, every night as I watched him on the ice or on TV, "That's my Colb, look at him go."

Although many of you didn't know of our story until April 7, 2020, it actually started in 2013, in a locker room in Swift Current, Saskatchewan. Looking back at the last 10 years had I known that I would eventually become Colby's widow less than 9 months after our dreams came true of us getting married, there is one thing that I'm certain of, I would have only run faster down the aisle to him.

CHAPTER 1

The Beginning of Us

I can only imagine what the locker room smelled like that day our story began, back in 2013. I mean, after many years of smelling Colby's hockey equipment, I'm confident it stunk in there. At the time, Colby was playing in the WHL for the Swift Current Broncos. I'm certain that amongst all the stench, there was music blasting and Colby was dancing and joking around with his teammates flashing that signature smile of his. He was having the time of his life. Living his dream. Getting to play the game that he loved so much with people that he loved just the same.

After the rink, he'd head home to his billet family. He'd go play with his little billet sister, Shayne, and his billet brother, Jace. He'd sit around the table that evening and chat about his upcoming game, with his billet parents, Kim and Brian. For those of you that don't know what a billet family is, they are a family that takes in hockey players so they have a place to live during the season. Most hockey players move away from their immediate family to a new city or sometimes even a new country, starting at the age of 15-16. Colby's billet family did more than just let him live with them during the hockey season. They made an everlasting impact on the man he became. They were absolutely some of the most important people in his life, and eventually mine. To call them anything but family would be a disservice to the way they loved us and the way that we loved them. Ok, back to the locker room. Before Colby left that day, he somehow came across my Instagram page on his home feed. He looked at one of his buddies and told him that I had immediately become his "Instagram crush" and that "I'm going to marry this girl one day". We hadn't met. I had zero idea who he was. And I was living in Ontario. But none of that mattered to Colb. He made his mind up that day and nothing was going to change it.

If we are being completely honest (and we are…) It took me a while to be convinced. He was living in another province. I really didn't know much about hockey (nor did I care to at the time.) And the idea of jumping into a long-distance relationship at such a young age sounded like a ton of work. So, I did what many girls would do in my situation. I just ignored his messages. I would read them. And I thought they were really sweet. I was flattered. But I didn't respond. I didn't respond for a long time. But he was persistent. So persistent that even though I never responded, he continued to message me for almost two years. It almost became comical. I mean, who does that? Who continues to message someone for so long and never gets the time of day? Colb does. That's who does.

Looking back, I often get angry with myself for not responding sooner. Don't get me wrong, I'll never doubt God's timing in it all, and to be honest, I probably wasn't ready to date when that first DM showed up. But goodness, I would have loved to have more time with him. Because the time that I did get with Colb here on earth will never feel like enough. I will always be longing for more.

When I finally did "cave" (pun intended), to one of his countless DM's, and we started talking, I could tell he was really special. And though it took two years to get me to respond, it only took a few weeks of talking to him for me to know that I had to meet him. So, I did what many would call crazy. I went for it. I booked a flight to visit him in Rhode Island where he was playing for the Boston Bruin's AHL team.

I'll never forget the day I met Colb in person. I don't know that I'd ever felt such excitement. The first time I saw him. Our first hug. Our first kiss- Colb's last first kiss. I get chills each time I think about it all. It wasn't an easy task for me to make the trip to see him. I was living at my parents' house in Barrie, Ontario at the time. I was still in school. He was in Rhode Island and on the road a ton, but I knew I had to make it happen. I knew I had to meet Colb.

So that morning I packed the biggest suitcase I owned and dragged it with me as I got on the GO Train for my two-hour ride to Toronto. I lugged it with me as I walked through the rush hour commute to get to campus. Remember, I was in school, and I had to go to class that day. Turns out that this would become a regular occurrence in the coming months. My professors and my classmates would know right away when I was flying to see Colb. Because here I'd come, every few weeks, dragging my 50-pound suitcase into class, only to jump on a flight as soon as class was over.

I remember taking off that afternoon on my flight from Toronto to Boston and having the realization that this trip could alter my life forever. I was nervous, anxious, excited, a little bit scared, and super happy all at the same time. I'm sure the passenger next to me could tell I was all nerves because I was visibly shaking the entire flight. When I landed in Boston, Colby would be there to pick me up. And in true Emily fashion, I was so nervous I walked right past him at arrivals. But he saw me and began yelling my name. As I turned around, he had the most beautiful smile I'd ever seen. He grabbed me, kissed me, and told me right there in the middle of the airport, "I'm going to marry you one day Emily."

I didn't know exactly what was planned that weekend, but I knew that I'd experience my first "game day." Colb had games that entire weekend and Friday night happened to be a home game and the first time I'd get to see if he was actually any good. Not that I'd have any idea if he was good. I mean, I knew that he was good considering the team he was on. But still, I was eager to see for myself. I found out pretty quickly that game day is more than just the game. I mean, it's an entire day. It starts around noon with his ever-important pregame lunch. Always chicken and pasta. Then there was the pregame nap. Then the wake-up call. Then the pump-up music in the shower. Then lay out the suit he'd wear that evening to the game. On this particular game-day, he asked me to pick his suit and tie. I didn't realize at that moment this would soon become a tradition in our home and that I'd be Colb's "suit picker" from here on out.

Honestly, as exciting as all of this was, I just wanted to be near him. I wanted to get to know him. I wanted to learn all that I could in the short time we had together. Yes, I was looking forward to watching him do his thing, but I couldn't wait for the game to be over so we could actually spend some time together. I came to see Colb the person, not Colb the hockey player. And though I knew that was a huge part of the person he is, the Colb that I was getting to know away from the ice was the one that I was quickly falling for.

I'd be lying if I said that I wasn't nervous about going to the game. I was for sure more nervous than Colb was. I mean, all he had to do was play. And that was super familiar to him. I on the other hand was walking into something so unfamiliar. So uncomfortable. So different than anything I'd ever been a part of. I'd sit with the other players' wives and girlfriends. I'd head down to the family room after the game to meet Colb. I felt so out of place that first night. I felt like I didn't belong. Little did I know that this place would soon become like a second home for me. So much so that a few years later, Colb would become the first Providence Bruin to have his number retired and hung from the rafters. And it wasn't just because of the hockey player he was. It was more about the person he was.

As awkward as that first night was, strangely, I didn't want it to end. I knew when it ended, it meant one day closer to me having to go home. To leave Colby. This was a short trip, I wanted so badly to pause time. Turns out that the following day was Valentine's Day. I don't know if that was fate or just chance, but I thought it was kind of fun that we'd be spending time together on a day that is so well known for being with the one you love. Speaking of fate, a couple of days later, my flight got canceled due to terrible weather in Canada, so we got to spend an extra 24 hours together. We joked around a little bit that we didn't think it was an accident and someone was looking out for us.

I did my best to play a little hard to get over the first weekend. I'm not sure how well I did but I sure didn't want him to think he'd completely won me over that quickly. But I was certain he was the one. The moment I left his side and got back home, I told anyone that would listen to me, I'd found my person and Colb was right, he was going to marry me one day.

CHAPTER 2

The Hockey Life

I'd only been home for about a week after our first weekend together when Colby called me and surprised me with a flight back to Providence. It was during that week, I got fully immersed in the crazy hockey lifestyle and all it entailed. The practices, the routines, the pregame naps, game days, travel days, the fans, etc. I had never experienced anything like this before. And to be honest, I knew absolutely nothing about hockey other than the team who got the most pucks into the net won. But I sure did love cheering Colb on. I just pretended I had a clue what was happening on the ice and after every game, I would tell him how well he played. I just assumed since I saw his number so much, it meant that he was playing well. Sometimes, according to Colb, that wasn't the case. It was one of the things he said he loved the most about me- the fact that I never knew if he actually played well or not. I just loved watching him play out his dream and I simply couldn't get enough of him.

It didn't take long for people to begin referring to us as the "Ginger Power Couple." And I kind of liked the sound of that. Over the next few months, I would fly back and forth as often as I could to visit Colby during his season. It was a lot to handle between my school and his insanely crazy schedule. But we were both all in and were willing to do whatever it took to be with each other as much as we could. We lived this lifestyle for two whole years, all

7

year round. We were becoming professionals at this long-distance relationship thing, and we always made the most of each moment we got to have together. Honestly, from the moment we met the first time, we learned to appreciate the time we had together and to make the most out of every trip because we knew it was short-lived. The irony of it all now…

After two years of back and forth, lots of prayers, and a ton of conversations with loved ones, I finally decided to put my career on hold and move to Providence to be with Colb full-time. It all felt surreal. I had a front-row seat to watch Colb live out his dream. We had become a part of an amazing hockey family. A family who I had no idea how badly I'd need in the coming season of life. Hockey life definitely consists of a brotherhood, that's easy to see. But what most don't get the chance to see is the sisterhood that develops away from the ice.

There is a stigma about hockey wives. None of us work. We are materialistic. And we are just coasting off our husbands' success. However, this is the farthest thing from the truth. Many of the hockey wives that I have the privilege to know are the strongest women in my life. Like myself, many of the wives I became friends with, sacrificed their careers and couldn't work because we were living in another country, or the travel didn't allow it. We all did this knowing that a hockey career doesn't last forever, and we were willing to set aside our dreams to support our boys following theirs. Many girls were learning a new language in a whole new country. Some had children and were raising them alone when the boys would go away on a long road trip. Some were still working and able to continue their careers all while managing to show up at every game in support of their husbands. I learned to lean on my hockey sisters very early on because unless you have been a part of the crazy hockey lifestyle- the last-minute moves, the calls up and down, the trades, waivers, the judgment from all those that aren't in your shoes- you don't really get it. These women got me, I got them, and they quickly became my people.

It really is interesting when you think about it. Yes, we were on the same team. Yes, we rooted for each other like crazy. But at the same time, all our boys were in the AHL, and they were competing against each other for the next spot in the NHL. This was a really big deal. Yet you'd never know it because of the way we all continued to show up for each other. Though I knew at the time how important our hockey family was to us, I had no idea how important they'd soon become.

We were also extremely fortunate during our time in Providence and Boston, to make friends outside of our hockey family. Two groups of friends that stand out most were the Fokin Family and our church friends. It was so healthy for both of us to have friends outside of hockey (as much as we loved them). It was nice to take a break from always talking about work or who was going to get the next call-up or anything hockey related for that matter. One of my best friends and bridesmaid, Kellie Fokin, and her family would invite Colby and myself to celebrate every holiday when we couldn't make it back to Canada. They became our family away from our family. It became a running inside joke at the Fokin House, that every time they had us over for dinner and drinks (grasshoppers were very common), Colb would get a text or a call that he was being called up to the NHL. Not only did their house become a comforting place for us to go and just be ourselves but it also became our "good luck" place for us as well.

Our church friends were no different. Colby never grew up going to church and really didn't care to attend until we started dating. Every Sunday that his schedule allowed, he would attend church with me. I will never forget the Sunday when Colby raised his hand and dedicated his life to the Lord. Another extremely proud moment for me. Colby always said that going to church changed his life. Our church friends loved, celebrated, and prayed for us through all our milestones and some of those friendships are still ones that I hold close to my heart and I know Colby appreciated so much.

Colby's dream of playing in the NHL would come true on December 21, 2017. Looking back on that day, it was all a whirlwind. He was at practice when his coach skated over to him and told him he needed to pack his stuff right away and get to Boston because he would be playing tonight. The problem was I'd just flown back home to Ontario for Christmas where Colb would meet us a few days later. But with this news, our plans quickly changed! I'll never forget that call from Colb announcing he'd been called up. I mean, the call only lasted about 3 minutes and I don't remember what I said, I just know there was a lot of screaming and shouting and celebrating and for sure some nerves from the both of us. I could tell he was so excited but could also feel all the other emotions from his end of the line. I mean, he'd worked his entire life for this moment, and he'd made it. He'd finally made it. Through all my excitement and even some tears, I realized I needed to hang up and figure out how to get back to Boston as soon as possible. He told me that he totally understood if I couldn't make it and I told him that there was no way that I was missing the game.

There are no words to describe the butterflies I felt for Colb during the flight. I was beaming with pride and there was nothing that could take the smile off my face. When I finally got to the rink and saw him skate out on the ice, I couldn't help but tear up. He was wearing #26. He picked that number because we were both born on the 26th. Him in December, me in April. If you have never been to TD Garden for a Bruins game and are a hockey fan, you need to go. Even if you don't love hockey, it's an experience. The atmosphere in the rink is known for being incredible, and I'm here to tell you that it's electric. When you're in the stands and the music starts and all the lights begin to flash, you can't help but get goosebumps. Now imagine watching your person skating out to play his first ever NHL game, oh the goosebumps. That night was one of the best nights of our lives, and one that I will cherish until my dying day.

Big things were happening off the ice as well. It was early June 2018, when I learned Colb planned to ask my dad if he could marry me. I knew my dad would be thrilled, but I was still super nervous leading up to that day. We all happened to be in Nashville at CMA Fest and Colb found a moment when the two of them could spend some alone time together. I remember sitting in our hotel room anxiously waiting for Colbs' return. I wanted to know everything. What did he say? How did he react? Was there any hesitation at all? I had so many things running through my mind and my heart. In the end, I don't remember asking him a single question. I just remember Colb walking into the room with a big grin on his face. He walked over to me and whispered, "I told you I was going to marry you, Emily."

I guess you could say we headed into the next hockey season on a "high." Everything was falling into place and things were looking up. Colby had made it and was playing in the NHL. We were engaged to be married. And on top of everything else, Colby got the call to take a once-in-a-lifetime trip with the Bruins to China. For those who don't know, this is a really big deal, and most teams and players never get to experience anything like this. But Colb did.

As great as everything was, the life of a professional athlete isn't as glamorous as most think. What people fail to see from the outside looking in, is all the ups and downs that come with being a part of a professional sports franchise. Colb and I were about to experience a ton of it in the coming year. Colb didn't make the Bruins right out of camp, so we'd be starting the season in Providence. He'd be called up here and there, but we were constantly on this roller coaster between Boston and Providence and most days we didn't know where we were going next.

Being a professional athlete, or a partner of one can be almost dehumanizing at times. People seem to forget these players actually have a life outside of the rink or stadium or arena. I realize for most people watching their favorite team can bring so much joy (or so much pain depending on the circumstances). Now imagine being a player. Or being a player's spouse or child. Imagine the emotions. The ups and downs. The pressure to perform night in and night out. The uncertainty of being called up and sent back down. I mean, that doesn't happen in most jobs. Imagine being a banker and one day finding out that you've been "sent down" to another branch. And then two weeks later sent back to your original branch and then three days later sent to yet another branch in another state or even another country.

When I tell you there were a lot of sleepless nights, it's an understatement. Yes, from the outside looking in, the life of a professional athlete looks pretty glamorous, but it comes with a ton of hard work and isn't always what it seems. And to be honest, the more Colbs' career grew and the more successful he became, we saw more people show up wanting more from us. Tickets, money, free gear, meet and greets with him and other famous players, the list goes on and on. Some days were really hard. And this isn't me looking for pity, this is me asking you all to think before you criticize next time you're at an event. I realize you paid good money for those seats. I realize you want to be entertained. And you deserve it. But I can promise you, those players are giving everything they've got and more to win the game. They sacrifice everything to be out there and if they mess up it was not intentional. They were trying so hard to win. They are trying so hard night in and night out not to let you or anyone else down. But they aren't puppets. They aren't robots. They aren't machines. They will fail at times. They will mess up now and then. Give them some grace. They are giving it their all. Just like you and I do in our jobs.

* * * * * * * * * * * * * * *

December 17, 2018. Almost a year after Colby made his NHL debut, another hockey dream of his would come true. Colb would score his first NHL goal against the Montreal Canadiens. One of my favorite Colb stories happened the night before with one of his best friends, Danton Heinen. It is not my story to tell but it makes me smile every single time. Just another example of how special the hockey brotherhood really is. I wasn't there to see it in person. I hated that I wasn't able to be there, but I was watching the game, sitting on our apartment room floor wrapping Christmas gifts. My neighbors above me, below me, and to the side of me, were probably wondering what the heck was happening as they heard screaming and jumping and shouting from our apartment. I waited up all night for Colby to get home from Montreal. I videoed him as he walked in the door and pulled the scoring puck out of his backpack. It is one of my favorite videos of Colb. He told me this would be the perfect addition to the man cave he'd dreamt of building one day.

January 1, 2019. Colby got to enjoy another experience of a lifetime when he played in the Winter Classic at Notre Dame Stadium. My parents had spent Christmas with us in Boston, so we flew out to Chicago to be with him and watch the game. We were so lucky my parents got to be part of another massive hockey milestone in Colby's career. We knew when we arrived there was a chance Colby might not play in the game. It was between Colby and Ryan Donato. I remember when Colby found out he was playing over Ryan and how guilty he felt for taking the spot. That was Colby in a nutshell. He always wanted the best for his teammate even if it meant they were playing over him. In a recent conversation that I had with Ryan, he told me he would give up that opportunity again and again for Colby in a heartbeat because of who Colby was as a teammate and person. Ryan was genuinely so happy for him. This also speaks on so many levels how respected

Colby was in the locker room. I have heard countless stories over the years, about how Colby would always text the person who beat him out of his spot and congratulate them. And we all know how much he truly meant it.

Soon after the Winter Classic, we knew we were about to go on waivers. For those of you that don't know what going on waivers means, it's when a player is being sent back down to the AHL. However, before you can "clear," all the other NHL teams have 24 hours to grab you. Or what they call, claim you. We knew multiple teams were interested in Colby. I remember sobbing the night before the last game in Boston. I headed to the game that night knowing I would have to say goodbye to all the girls on the team, all their families, and all our friends. I didn't want to leave Boston, our friends, our apartment, or our church. We had built an incredible life there. We had settled in, and we both loved our routine. But this is the business side of hockey life most don't see.

What I'd expected to be an exciting few months for us, with our wedding just around the corner, turned into an extremely stressful and challenging time. The magnitude of both personal and hockey stress we were under was absolute insanity. Something only the people who we knew and trusted the most would help us through. Colby would wake up the next morning and have to go to the rink, I would stay at home, and continue to pack not knowing where we were about to move. Waiver pick-ups are always posted on Twitter, at the same time, every single day. I was on FaceTime with my parents when my Dad announced (as they were refreshing Twitter) that Colby had been picked up by the Edmonton Oilers. "Emily, you are moving to Edmonton." Twitter told us we were moving back to Canada.

I remember having waves of emotions. Colby was still at the rink, packing up his gear, talking to the media about now being an Edmonton Oiler, and saying goodbye to his Boston Bruins teammates. He called me on his way back to the apartment and said, "I am on a plane in two hours. I need to be in Vancouver tonight."

Yup, you read that right! He came home, packed one suitcase, and left for the airport. One of the Bruins' girlfriends came over and helped me pack up our apartment in Boston. We then drove all the belongings from that apartment to our apartment in Providence. Within two days, I moved out of two apartments and was on a flight with six massive suitcases, carrying everything we owned, to Edmonton.

We were still a few months away from our wedding. Due to personal reasons, we now had to start from scratch. All the planning I'd done was for nothing. I had less than 6 months to plan a whole new wedding. I was in a brand new city, knew absolutely no one, and somehow had to plan the biggest day of our lives. That being said, the best part of the hockey sisterhood is as soon as you meet the girls at the first home game, you are welcomed immediately, and they become your new support system. They grabbed me by the hand and helped me through everything. I'm so grateful for each one of those ladies.

CHAPTER 3

Till Death Do Us Part

July 19, 2019.

The day our dreams came true.

The day also consisted of record-breaking heat and damaging winds.

But as I said, it was the day our dreams came true.

We danced. We laughed. We cried. It was perfect.

As I look back on that day, there are so many things which bring me comfort. I'm so grateful for all the pictures and videos we have. At the time, I remember being slightly annoyed and thinking it was a little excessive but, in the end, I wouldn't change it for anything. All we have are pictures and memories of our loved ones. That being said, if you are reading this and are engaged, or ever plan to be, get someone to film your wedding. Whether you hire someone or have a friend do it, film your wedding. You won't ever regret having that done. Just trust me on this one. I promise you you're going to want the video.

Another thing from our wedding day that is so comforting to me is the letter that Colb wrote to me the morning of our wedding. For those who have never read it before, this seems like the perfect time.

To my Beautiful Bride: Wow, I have been looking forward to this day since June 16 of last year. Em, today is the day that we finally get to say, "I do" and make us officially lifelong partners. I could have not found a more perfect person to marry than you. You are beautiful, you are genuine, you make me laugh, and you broaden my mind to so much more than I could ever imagine. This is it! We finally have the beginning of our lives together! Having children, celebrating anniversaries, getting to call you "wifey", there are so many things that I could write down because I am so excited to be your husband. Who would've thought a little persistence on Insta would've turned out to be the best thing to happen to us. Emily Lillian Jean Cave. Wow, it just sounds so perfect. The moment we get to kiss and walk down the aisle is something we will cherish forever. You are my everything, my beautiful bride, my #1 fan, my avocado toast eating, Starbucks drinking, redheaded smoking hot soon-to-be wife, and I cannot wait. I am your #1 fan and will be for as long as we live. I cannot wait to sit down, look across the table, and see my beautiful wife. You are my pride and joy and thank you so much for everything you've done to make this day so perfect. I love you with all my heart, Em. AGAPE.

When I say I was so lucky to get to marry that man, it's an understatement. He truly was the best thing to ever happen to me.

The pictures. The wedding video. Colb's note to me the morning of our wedding. And our vows. Those are the biggest things from that day I'll always hold close to my heart. We chose to write our own vows and here is what Colb said:

Emily Lillian Jean, (Colb begins crying) I didn't even last the first word. My Unicorn, my amazing, beautiful, redheaded Unicorn. (Keeps crying and says under his breath… get it together man.) You may think I overuse this term but there is way more to it than referring to a mythical creature. A Unicorn is described as a symbol of purity and grace, and I could not find a more relatable description of who you are as a person. You are always putting other people before yourself, and I am always amazed at how you do it with such humility. You take my breath away every time I stare into those beautiful brown eyes. And I even get a smile when you crack your hips in an awkward yet graceful way. You are there for me through the tough times. You are there to celebrate through the good. You are everything that I could imagine in a wife, and I cannot believe that I get to marry you. That is why I call you my Unicorn and I will be faithful to you for as long as we both shall live. 6 years ago, I laid eyes on you for the first time. I remember thinking to myself, this is what perfection looks like. I said to my buddies, I am going to marry that girl one day. Never in my wildest dreams did I think I would get the opportunity to say I do with you, and here we are. The cliche everything happens for a reason, can never be more fitting. You motivate me to be better at every aspect of my life. A better person. A better life partner. A better hockey player. A better role model. I would not be anywhere I am today without you, and I will spend the rest of my life showing you how thankful I am to have you as my wife. Before God, family, and friends, I am here to say, you are my everything Emily, and I cannot wait to spend eternity with you. Em, I promise to be there for you when you need a hug. I promise to be there for you when you are hungry for avocado toast. I promise to support you when you need someone in your corner. I promise to help you develop your many gifts. I promise to listen and validate you when we express our feelings. I promise to be a loving and caring Father to our children. And I promise to be the loving and faithful husband that you deserve. You have sacrificed so much for me, and I am forever grateful for everything you have ever done and will do for me. I promise to be everything you have ever imagined in a husband. I love you. Agape.

Both of our love languages were words of affirmation. The letters we wrote to each other on our wedding morning along with our vow books are in a memory box full of letters and cards we wrote to each other over the years. Whether we were celebrating something special like our wedding, or it was a random day, we always took the opportunity to tell each other how much we loved and appreciated each other. Our wedding day was no different.

I loved Colby's words that day. So much so, I have his handwriting tattooed on my arm. It's just another beautiful reminder of how much that man loved me and how much I still love him.

A mentor of mine recently told me, "I don't know why this has happened to you but when it comes to your identity on this particular point, I need you to know this...you are still his wife. He picked you, over anyone and everything else. Just because he is gone doesn't mean that the role you earned was taken away. Nobody can remove that identity from you."

I remind myself of this on the hard days that no one can take away the fact that Colby picked me out of 7 billion people on the planet to spend the rest of his life with.

When we said "till death do us part" that day, we had no idea the heaviness of those words and how quickly death would come knocking on our door.

268 days. That's all we had left.

Knowing the outcome, I'd still say yes all over again. Colby fulfilled his vow to love me for the rest of his life, and as he said, "I can't wait to spend eternity with you." I will continue to fulfill my vow and love him for the rest of my life until we are reunited again. I can't wait to spend eternity with him.

CHAPTER 4

268 Days

After our wedding, we headed back to Boston to finish training for the rest of the summer. I remember as we were packing up our apartment during our last week in Boston feeling extra emotional about leaving. I just had an unsettling feeling about leaving Boston. At our last church service, I sobbed uncontrollably and just kept saying how I didn't want to leave. I had no idea at the time, but this would be Colby's and my last time together in the city where it all began for us. Last time at our favorite restaurants, last time at our church, last time with our Boston friends, last time at Boston Logan- the airport where he grabbed my face and kissed me and told me he was going to marry me.

We didn't know what we didn't know and though we were leaving Boston, our hope was we'd be back at some point. We had started talking about starting a family and how great it would be if we could have our baby in Boston the following summer because that is where we wanted to settle down, even after the hockey life was over. So as strange as it may sound, even though we were moving for the 19th time in 22 months, everything seemed to be falling into place. Everything seemed to be going perfectly. But I just couldn't shake that unsettling feeling. Our pastor, met with me before we left to go back to Edmonton and reminded me, "Emily, you are Graced for this." I didn't know at the time how much I'd lean on those words in the coming months.

We didn't expect it to happen so quickly, but Colby and I got pregnant right away. It was about a week before training camp started, and I got to deliver the news to Colby. The joy on his face when he found out was so special. I'll never forget that moment. We happened to be renting an Airbnb and Colb decided to tape both positive pregnancy tests above the bathroom mirror, so we'd be reminded each time we entered how blessed we really were. We had already picked out baby names and we started making bets on what the gender would be. I even began to buy baby things. One was a hospital bag that I still have. We both were just beaming with joy.

But a few weeks later, before we could even tell all our loved ones, the unimaginable happened. About 6 weeks after celebrating with Colb that we were going to be parents; I had a miscarriage. Colby just held me on the couch after practice the day we found out. We just held each other and cried. We felt like we were on such a high and everything was working out perfectly. And then this happened. This is something that I rarely talk about. I don't know that I had a ton of time to even grieve this loss because it would only be a short while later that I'd lose Colby too. It does bring me some joy knowing that Colby is up in Heaven, taking care of our baby. And I like to think they are both looking down on me cheering me on. There are so many days I wish Colby and I had a rainbow baby before he passed away. I would have given anything to get to watch him be a daddy. I will always long for a piece of Colb here on earth. A mini him. A little redhead just like the both of us. Maybe they would have had Colb's tiny ears. Maybe they would have had my big eyes. I will always wonder. I will always feel that secondary loss.

Although nothing can take away the pain of a miscarriage, Colby tried his best to ease some of it. For years, I begged Colby to get a dog, but he always wanted to wait until we were more settled. However, a few days after I miscarried, sitting in a Starbucks, Colby looked at me with teary eyes and said, "We are getting a dog." And then came Chester.

Colby would get sent to play in Bakersfield, California, a few days after we got Chester and because Chester didn't have all his shots yet, we couldn't fly him into the States. I flew Chester (8 weeks old) to my parent's house in Barrie, Ontario. I would later fly to Bakersfield to help Colby get settled into yet another brand new city. We wouldn't be in California long (like two weeks) before Colby got sent back to Edmonton. We were used to being called up and sent down in Boston, but Providence was less than an hour's drive away. Edmonton's AHL team was in a completely different country and time zone. The call-ups and down took more of a toll, human ping pongs, back and forth. We were in and out of hotels and team apartments with a brand-new puppy.

One time in particular, I landed in one city and had my phone turned off during the flight and when I turned my phone back on, Colby was already on another flight back to where I had just come from. So, I turned right back around. However, throughout all the craziness Colby stayed kind, patient, hardworking, and humble. Even those words don't say enough to describe him. He had an effortless ability to calm my nerves and make me laugh when I just wanted to cry. He knew how I was feeling and what I was thinking sometimes even before I did. We continued to make it work. We looked at the positives every single day. We continued to live out our daily motto, "be somebody that makes everybody feel like a somebody". We enjoyed every moment together of our newly married life despite the chaos.

It was during Colby's time in Bakersfield, that one of the most "famous" stories about him happened. Colby got into a fight and knocked out his opponent. After the game, Colby tracked down the guy's number and texted him to see if he was doing okay. The following day the opponent would post the text on social media, and it was at that moment the world got to see a glimpse of the man my husband was.

For the next few months, we would be living like human ping pong balls. However, I remember our last Christmas together being so special. Colby and I had a tradition when we were setting up our Christmas tree for every ornament that we put on the tree, we would tell the other person why we loved each other. We would play Christmas music. Christmas cookies would be baking in the oven and there may have been some rum and eggnogs too.

Though we barely had any furniture in our apartment in Bakersfield, we still went out and bought a Christmas tree because we couldn't break the tradition- especially because it was our first Christmas as a married couple. Even as I write this, I can't believe we only got to have one Christmas together as a married couple. It just doesn't seem fair. We would spend our actual Christmas break (which consisted of two days) with my family on Vancouver Island. We have so many special memories of that Christmas my family will forever hold onto. I don't know if I'd have done anything differently had I known it was going to be our last. It was beautiful just as it was.

Colby's birthday is the day after Christmas, and we spent that day traveling back to Bakersfield. There just happened to be an extremely rare snowstorm in California that year and we, some teammates, one of the girlfriends on the team and Chester ended up getting stuck for eight hours trying to drive from Los Angeles, jammed in a rental car. This is how Colby spent his last birthday on this earth. Sometimes, it hurts my heart to think that. However, I remember how much we laughed during the car ride. I remind myself it wouldn't have been a classic day in the life of Em and Colb, had the day gone smoothly. We were constantly having something happen to us, but we always made the most of it. After a really long day of travel and an intense hockey practice, we were finally able to celebrate Colb. Just Colby, Chester, and me. He opened his cards and gifts, and, in my card, I wrote about how excited I was to hopefully see him as a baby daddy for his next birthday.

A few days later the new year would come. It was 2020 and we had plans for it to be our best year yet. But sometimes our plans aren't God's plans. Sometimes the plans we make or the plans we dream up don't seem to work out the way we'd hoped for. 2020 would turn into the hardest and most confusing year of my life. But not yet. Colb was still here, and we were going to celebrate by ringing in the new year with the team surrounded by people we loved.

A few weeks later we headed to Palm Springs for All-Star Break with a group of teammates. During that trip, Kobe Bryant passed away in a helicopter crash. We spent the entire drive talking about how horrible his death was and how shocking it was for the sports fan community. I remember thinking about his wife Vanessa and wondering how she was. Never could I have ever imagined I would be in her shoes so soon.

The rumblings of the Global Pandemic and Covid started to increase over the next few weeks. There were talks about lockdowns and the season going on hold. No one had any idea of the impact and everything that was about to happen. From what the media was saying, if you were young and healthy, you were good. And Colby and I were both of those things. At this point, all we were told was that Covid was only seriously impacting elderly people or people at risk. We didn't see this as a huge threat to us, but we did worry about some of our loved ones and wanted to make sure we did all we could to keep our distance from anyone that Covid could really affect.

March 7th, 2020. This was the last hockey game Colby ever played. Normally at home games, the wives and girlfriends in Bakersfield would sit in a box. However, for some reason that game,

I decided to sit a few rows up from the bench with a few of my girlfriends. In all the years of Colby playing hockey, I had never sat so close to the bench or the ice. I remember telling the other girlfriends how loud it was and how cool it was that you could hear everything going on so close to the ice. I remember thinking Colby might see me, and it might make him nervous, but it turns out that he never even noticed I was there because he was so focused on the game! He scored a goal in that game. His last goal. In his final game. I screamed and cheered so loud, I caught one of the staff members' attention on the bench. The staff member told Colby during the intermission how excited I was for him, and Colby told him that he was so bummed he didn't see my reaction. We never thought anything of it. We just assumed there would be more goals and more games. But this was the last one. I had devoted years of my life to watching his games, and if I had just known this was his last game… I would have made the biggest sign in the world. I would have worn his jersey. I would have taken in the way his hair smelt after he put his gel in it. I would have cherished our tradition of me always picking out his game day suits. If only I'd have known.

March 11th, 2020. Colby had to leave to go on a road trip even though we knew the season was about to end. I woke up in tears that morning. I was petrified. The pandemic was getting worse, and we still didn't know who or what was safe. I told Colby, multiple times, I had a sick feeling that he was going to die. I told him not to board the plane and he couldn't leave me. He reassured me it was fine and all the media and scariness from Covid was probably taking a toll on me. He had gone on so many road trips over the years and I should have been used to this. However, this trip just felt different, and had a horrible gut feeling he was going to die. I still have the text messages on his phone from that day. He was sitting on the plane about to take off with his teammates.

Me - *"I literally feel sick to my stomach you're going to die."*
Colb - *"Baby, I am so sorry, but I promise you I am okay. I love you. Just pulling onto the runway. I will text you in Phoenix. Agape."*

As soon as they landed, the season would go on hold. The team flew home, and we all tried to figure out what to do next. Some people fled California right away, especially if they weren't from the States. People hustled to get back to their home countries before the borders closed. We felt torn. We didn't have our own house back in Canada. We were in the process of buying a place in Boston but because we were both Canadian, we wanted to get back on home soil but at the same time we didn't want to be "stuck" anywhere. As all this was going down, I became really sick. We thought it was Covid and were petrified. The team doctor tested me, and we decided to stay in California until my results came back. It took 17 days for my Covid results to come back- they would be negative and instead, it turned out to be Valley Fever from the poor air quality in Bakersfield.

During those 17 days, as we waited on those results, some of the conversations that happened cannot be explained other than some weird sort of… "fate." I hate to call it that, but I can't think of another way to say it. We decided to choose a long Netflix series to watch because we knew we couldn't do anything else, and we had so much time to kill. We picked Grey's Anatomy. We watched episode after episode, about death, dying, and being sick. We started having all these "hypothetical" conversations that normal newlyweds wouldn't have in their mid-twenties. There was one episode during season two where a young girl had got a pole stuck through her during a train crash and she wasn't going to make it. Her fiancé was trying to get there in time before she was going into surgery, but they couldn't wait any longer. Dr. McDreamy asked the girl what she wanted him to tell her fiancé when he saw him. She answered, "If love was enough, I'd still be there with you."

I looked over at Colby, teary-eyed, and I asked him what he would say to me if he couldn't say goodbye. I asked him what message he would give to the hypothetical Dr. McDreamy to tell me. He didn't respond for a few minutes then he started to tear up. He said he had no idea and couldn't fathom having to decide what his last words would be to me. We continued to watch the episode and about 10 minutes later, he looked over and told me what he would say. I remember it vividly. He put my hair behind my ear, and he told me how much he loved me. He told me how he would always be with me, and that he was so proud of me. And then he said, "Em, that is never going to happen. We are going to have a daughter named Charlie (it was the girl's name we picked out), a son, and adopt a child from Haiti too. We're going to grow old together." Colby never got to tell me his last words during the four days he was in the hospital. I have to believe, we watched that episode and I asked that question, and Colby answered it how he did, because I was going to need those words one day.

Another thing we talked about during our Grey's Anatomy binge-watching was organ donations and funeral arrangements. Again, not conversations that you expect to be having at our age, but also really important things to talk about for all married couples. We didn't have a will which has created a lot of problems and heartache for me even almost three years later. However, we both told each other our wishes that day. We both wanted to be organ donors and we both wanted to be cremated. Looking back now, I do believe in a weird and sick and twisted way, I was being prepared. Being prepared to have to make these decisions I should never have had to make. Being prepared to not be able to be with Colb when he passed or even get to say a proper goodbye. I believe what Colb said to me on that random day is exactly what he would have told me if he could've said goodbye. But most importantly, I believe what the young girl in the episode said, if love was enough, Colb would still be here with me.

CHAPTER 5

Oh, Canada

As soon as my Covid results came back negative we booked a flight back to Ontario to quarantine at my parent's house. My parents had a finished apartment in their basement, and we felt safe and comfortable doing our quarantine there. We also thought that if we did eventually get to Boston for the summer, it was closer for us to travel from there. My parents prepared for our arrival by stocking up the basement with food, board games, cards, coloring books, wine (lots of wine), and dog toys for Chester. We packed up our lives in California and I took a video of Colby and Chester on our last walk around our neighborhood. I captioned it, "One last California stroll." Little did I know...

April 2, 2020. My parents arranged a whole caravan parade to get us home safely when we landed in Canada. Because we were arriving from another country, we had to begin our mandatory 14-day quarantine as soon as we arrived. However, we also needed to get home somehow. We had 3 different families in 3 different vehicles come and pick us up. When we walked outside of the airport, they were all holding Canadian flags from their cars and welcoming us home. Of course, we couldn't hug any of them or give anyone a proper greeting. So, we just loaded up all their trunks with our stuff. My Dad was in the car that Colby and I would be driving so he jumped in the other car with my Mom. My parents had loaded our car with all our favorite Canadian snacks. Tim Hortons, smarties, all the good stuff. Oh, and two water bottles. The water bottle on Colby's side of the car still stays there to this day- unopened. My parents and I do not have the heart to remove it from the car.

We felt so relieved to be back on Canadian soil and hunkered down to begin our mandatory quarantine. For the next four days, we continued to watch Grey's Anatomy. We would get fresh air in my parent's backyard. We played with Chester. We played cards and board games. We colored in our coloring books. We FaceTimed family and friends. And we went through some of my old baby books. We were still trying for our rainbow baby all while actively planning to take a trip to Haiti to visit an orphanage over there for our first wedding anniversary. We were living in a global pandemic, and life was so uncertain for everyone. And we had no idea that our world was about to come crashing down.

CHAPTER 6

14 Hours

It was a Monday- my last full day with Colby.

Monday, April 6, 2020. The last morning that I would wake up to Colby and those words, "Good Morning Em. I love you".

We had a rule that before we looked at our phones in the morning, we had to say "Good Morning. I love you" to each other. Colby was way better at it than I was. He was always so good at being present and real in each and every moment. Had I known that was our last morning together, I would have said so many more things.

Probably something along the lines of "Good Morning. I love you so much. Thank you for changing my life. Thank you for giving me a life that everyone deserves. Thank you for always putting me first. You are my best friend, my whole heart. You have brought me so much happiness and I will forever be grateful for you, Colb. Our love is the greatest love I have ever known. Please don't leave me. I can't do this without you. I am not strong enough. Agape." And I would have said it a million times and then a million more.

Unfortunately, we are trained to believe that in life we are guaranteed all this time. Newly married, and in our mid-twenties, and we thought we were invincible. Yet that morning we were experiencing our last hugs, last cuddles, and last kisses. You hear it said all the time - you never know when the last time is going to be the last time. And you don't even think about it until it's too late. So, before you keep reading, here is your reminder to live today as if it were the last with the person you love the most. You won't ever regret doing that.

Colby would get up before me and make himself a coffee. He would also make my morning tea since I'm not a coffee drinker and we would go about starting our day. We spent the majority of that day having our typical everyday moments together- joking around, laughing, listening to music, playing with Chester, and planning for our future. Looking back, those everyday moments are some of my favorite memories and some of the moments I miss the most. The intimate, quiet, and what I thought were "boring" moments, that no one else would see. Memories I never thought would matter in those moments, but I find myself constantly replaying them now. I took them for granted because I thought we were guaranteed all this time together. We were naive and thought our lives were just beginning when in reality, Colb was dying, and he was dying incredibly fast. It makes me sick to my stomach to think about it.

We were a few days into our quarantine in my parent's basement, but we were making the most of it. Other than the whole quarantine and the whole world shutdown aspect- life seemed to be going really well for us. It was a nice day outside so Colby took his golf clubs to the backyard to get some fresh air and I joined him. He was wearing a Nike hat and a red plaid hoodie jacket- a jacket that still hangs in my closet to this day. He would hit golf balls and Chester would chase after them and bring them back to him. I remember thinking how cute it was, so I began to video it all. Little did I know, this would be one of the last videos that I have of Colby. Eventually, we would go back down to the basement, and Colby would change into workout clothes. Although the hockey season was on pause, he was still doing the workouts being sent to players by their trainers to stay in shape. He wanted to be ready to go when he got the call saying the season was starting up again. It was his contract year, he was playing amazingly, and he didn't want to jeopardize his contract signing for the upcoming summer. Colby completed his full workout outside in the backyard. My parents watched from their backroom window. My Mom has a photo of Colby smiling and waving to her as he was doing the stairs. After he was done, he came back in, showered up, and got ready for an IG live interview with one of our Hillsong church friends. Again, there wasn't a sign that anything was remotely wrong. We had a salad for dinner that night. Colby's last meal was a salad in a black plastic bowl. Had I just known that was our last meal together, we would have not been having a healthy salad in a plastic bowl. We would have had his favorite meal, drinks, and lots of desserts because Colb had the biggest sweet tooth. But instead, our last dinner date was a boring salad.

After we ate, Colby did his IG live interview. He talked about so many things going on in his life. I feel like followers who tuned in that night saw a bit of the Colby, I fell in love with, not just the hockey player but the person. He talked about his faith, a bit about hockey, our life in Boston, our wedding, Chester, and funny stuff he had done in the past. I remember his smile during the whole interview- his big famous smile talking about all the things and people he loved in his life. After the interview was done, Colby would check his phone to see a missed call from Keith Gretzky. Keith was calling to tell him when the season restarted, he would be going to play with the Oilers in the Stanley Cup playoffs. This was the last call Colby got. I remember us talking about how cool the Stanley Cup playoffs would be. We were thinking about all the possibilities of how the NHL would host them with the pandemic and restrictions. We even made a joke about getting a wedding ring and Stanley Cup ring all within a year. Life seemed good, really good.

Shortly after that conversation, everything started to change. I remember Colby going to the bathroom to get ready for bed and coming back not looking well. He was pale and just seemed off. You have to keep in mind, this was the first time EVER, in all the years we had been together I had seen Colby sick. He was the epitome of health. He was under 10% body fat. He never got a cold, the flu, stomach bugs, anything. This was completely out of his character. I remember having this sinking feeling in my stomach something was seriously wrong. I originally thought maybe he had gotten Covid. I was worried sick and didn't know what we should do. We were still in our quarantine period and doctors were only doing online appointments unless you were dying.

Colby reassured me he didn't have Covid and he was just really tired, so we decided to curl up on the couch and throw on an episode of Grey's Anatomy. It was during that episode, the sinking feeling in my stomach grew worse and worse. He just didn't look well so we decided to turn off the episode and try to go to bed.

11:36 pm. Colby started to complain about a headache. I looked at him and said, "Colby, what if it is a brain tumor?" He reassured me once again he was fine and there is no way it could be a brain tumor. He told me, "It is probably just a migraine." To which I responded, "Colb, you don't get migraines".

However, after googling his symptoms, and with Colb's reassurance, I tried to convince myself it was just a migraine. But my heart and gut knew it wasn't just a migraine. For the next couple of hours, Colby would be in extreme pain with horrible headaches, and he would puke four times. After each time, we would crawl back into bed and eventually fall back asleep. "It's just a migraine," he kept telling me. Just a migraine.

6:30 am. I rolled over to see Colby in a state I will never forget. No words will be able to describe this. And no amount of therapy will ever take away the trauma I witnessed. As I rolled over to see if he was awake and ask him how he was feeling, I put my hand on his face, my palm on his cheek, my four fingers by his ear, and my thumb tucked underneath his ear. Just as if I was going to roll over and kiss him. He was completely hypothermic. His skin color was ghost white. I had never witnessed anything like it. I frantically started yelling his name. At that moment, I thought he was already gone. He managed to mumble a reply. I told him that I was going to get help and not to move. My fear and gut feeling were right, this was not just a migraine.

I ran to the bathroom and grabbed toilet gloves, I threw on a mask and sprinted upstairs to my parents' room. They are in their late 60s, so I was worried about giving them Covid since we still had no idea if Colby had Covid or not. I stood at their bedroom door, 6 feet away, and I yelled, "something is wrong with Colby". They quickly jumped out of bed, but we remained 6 feet apart. They immediately started making calls to the health lines and the local hospital. It was all happening so fast. No one wanted to take him because of the fear of Covid and the fact we had just gotten back from the States. As my parents were making calls, I ran back downstairs to check on Colby. He was still laying there. His mumbling was getting worse. I told him we were calling for help. I went back upstairs to provide an update to my parents. He wasn't getting better. He was getting worse. We needed to call an ambulance immediately. When I ran back down, Colby had managed to somehow get up from our bed, puking everywhere, and stumble to the back family room. He was now passed out on the couch. He was completely naked and had peed all over the couch. At this point, I couldn't get any response from him. All I could do was scream at my parents we needed help right away.

I remember the paramedics arriving. I remember being pushed out of their way as they started working on him. I remember trying to tell them what had happened all while trying to process it myself. I remember having to remind myself to breathe. They would not allow my parents to come downstairs. It was all happening so fast.

They were all gowned up, with masks, face shields, and gloves. The first stretcher wouldn't fit through the back door, so they had to put him in a stretcher that folded up like a chair. As they carried him up the back stairs, I watched Colby's head bobbing and his eyes rolling back. I remember seeing neighbors watching from their windows as they loaded him into the ambulance. I remember asking the paramedics to take me with them. I needed to be by his side. I needed to tell the doctors and nurses what had happened. They told me the best they could do with Covid restrictions was to have me write the symptoms, his health card number, and my cell phone number on a sticky note and they would give it to his doctor.

At this point, I was still trying to stay 6 feet away from my parents. I was standing at the end of their driveway alone, staring at the ambulance that was just sitting there. Why wasn't it moving? Why weren't they in a hurry? What was happening to Colby? I looked back at my parents. Then I looked back at the ambulance and lost it. I just started yelling.

"Why aren't you moving? Why aren't your sirens on? What is taking so long?"

Colby was dying. And no one seemed to care. I collapsed onto my knees. And I overheard my Mom say, "Screw Covid, we have to go hug her."

Once the ambulance finally drove away, my Mom helped me back to my feet. It could have been 5 minutes, could have been 35 minutes, could have been an hour. I don't remember. But we eventually made it back inside where I started frantically making calls. Calls to family members, the NHL, Colby's agent, etc. It was so hard because I couldn't provide them with much information other than the fact that Colby was taken to the hospital and was not in a good state. I remember so many of them sounding hopeful, but my heart and gut knew, this was not good.

One of the calls I made was to one of my best friends, Alex. She was one of our bridesmaids but also a paramedic. My Mom suggested I call to ask her if she knew anyone working at the hospital who would be able to provide me with an update. She hung up quickly and started making calls. Not long after, I got in contact with the emergency doctor through one of her friends. He told me that I needed to get to the hospital immediately as they had just discovered fluid in Colby's brain (what they thought could be blood) on a CT scan. He also told me that Colby would need to be airlifted to Sunnybrook Hospital in Toronto for emergency brain surgery.

The local hospital is about a 6-minute drive from my parent's place. When I arrived, they were getting ready to put Colby into a medically induced coma and fly him to Toronto. Before they did, I quickly got to go in and see him. He couldn't respond but I told him that I loved him. I held his hand and kissed him. I told him that I was going to be right back, and that they just needed to put him to sleep for a bit but I would see him when he woke up after surgery. I left the room, and they began to prep him. I watched from behind the glass while begging his medical team to let me go with him on the helicopter. Of course, due to Covid, I was not allowed to. I sat on the hospital hallway floor with my parents by my side and sobbed. I wasn't allowed back into his room after they intubated him. It felt like we waited a lifetime for them to carry him out to the ambulance and drive him to the helicopter pad. Meanwhile, I was frantically trying to update people and make calls. My phone wouldn't stop ringing. The word was getting out about what was happening. Looking back, I have no idea how I did it all. Eventually, my parents would step in and take my phone away because I couldn't explain anything to anyone without losing it.

I remember when they finally told us they were going to move him. I was on the phone with a family member, and I saw them as they began wheeling his intubated body right to me so I could touch him one last time. I dropped my phone to the ground and started screaming. This could not be happening to me. I held onto his body as tightly as I could, I didn't want to let go. The transfer team told me they had to go and pulled me off him because time was crucial, and they needed to get him to Toronto.

My parents and I rushed out of the hospital. And while pulling out of the parking lot, we stopped on the side of the road by the helicopter pad. I wanted to watch Colby being transported out of the ambulance and onto the helicopter. I needed to watch him take off and make sure he got safely on the helicopter. Once the helicopter took off, we raced back home to pack a few bags as quickly as we could and get to Sunnybrook Hospital in Toronto.

The next 30 minutes are all a blur. I was throwing our clothes into bags for the hospital and making calls to as many people as I could. The few conversations that I remember having were with Colby's billet parents Kim and Brian, Julie Cassidy (the wife of the Bruins head coach), Wendy Tippett (the wife of the Oilers head coach), and Kelly Backes (the wife of David Backes). I told them that they needed to let his teammates know what was happening before they found out through the media. I knew that I needed to make a public statement while Colby was in the helicopter to Sunnybrook for the Oilers to post. I was in a complete state of shock.

However, I have this one vivid memory that gives me chills thinking back on all that went down in those 30 minutes. As I was packing, my Mom came downstairs, I looked her in the eyes and said, "I am going to have to pick out an outfit for my husband's funeral."

As we were loading the car, I got a phone call from one of the critical care doctors in Toronto. They told me that Colby just landed and that they were rushing him into surgery. I replied, "Do everything that you can to keep him alive" and then walked outside and got into my parent's car.

The drive seemed to go fast, maybe it was my phone blowing up from family, friends, and teammates because of the public statement being released. Or it could have been the calls with NHL doctors asking for updates. Or maybe it was my parents trying to reassure me that everything was going to be okay. But as we arrived at Sunnybrook Hospital I knew that my whole life was about to forever change.

My parents and I met a hospital worker at the front door. They told us they could only escort me to the critical care waiting room. Covid restrictions were intense, and they just wouldn't allow anyone else in the hospital. My parents just stood at the front door of the hospital and watched me walk inside with the worker. I can only imagine the fear that they saw in my eyes as I walked away. I know I could feel the fear with every bone in my body. I arrived at the critical care waiting room and sat all alone. It was small, very small, with only a handful of chairs. I'll never forget that room. And to this very day, I could draw you a picture of every chair and side table exactly as they appeared that day. I sat there for almost an hour all alone, waiting to hear if my 25-year-old husband was still alive. I rocked myself back and forth in the hospital chair. It was in that chair I vowed to Colby and myself, no matter the outcome, our story wasn't going to end in the hospital. I would continue to be his "little world changer". I listened repeatedly to our Christian worship playlist. One song in particular, Waymaker. It would be those lyrics I would use to make my first quote on Instagram telling the world that Colby was in the hospital.

"Last night, and today have been the worst days of my life. Colby is currently in surgery, and they are fighting to keep him alive. We need a miracle. Please pray for my husband and best friend." Way maker, MIRACLE WORKER. Promise keeper, light in the darkness. My God, that is who you are.

Then it happened. The door finally opened and in walked Colby's medical team. He was out of surgery. What happened next... there are no words. I was sitting there all alone. 26 years old. Just married. Exactly 14 hours after Colby first complained about a headache. They said he had a colloid cyst. I was right, it was a brain tumor. A colloid cyst is a fluid-filled sac that forms in the brain, usually in the third ventricle. In other words, a non-cancerous brain tumor. Although they had managed to remove the cyst successfully, it had grown so big it shifted, and his brain had filled with spinal fluid. This explains why he was in so much pain the night before. It also explains the fluid they originally saw on the first CT scan. The prognosis for Colby wasn't good. Within 14 hours of what Colby thought was just a migraine, I was told he most likely would never wake up again. I will never forget the neurosurgeon talking to me. He was folding his scrub cap in his hands. I could tell he was struggling to make eye contact with me. If I were to ever hold a scrub cap, I could show you exactly how he was folding it. Accompanying the neurosurgeon was a critical care doctor, critical care nurse, critical care floor manager, and a spiritual counselor.

26 years old. All alone. Hearing the worst possible news I could ever hear. In medical terms that were way above my head. Somehow, I still knew what they were saying- my husband needed a miracle, or he was not going to make it. 14 hours. That is all it took for my whole world to come crashing down. I asked to see Colby. I begged them. I told them they could put me in a diaper and I wouldn't leave his room. I didn't need to eat or drink anything. I just needed to be with him. Again, because of Covid restrictions, I was told I would not be allowed to see him.

How could this be happening? My 25-year-old husband was dying, and I wasn't even allowed to hold his hand or be in the same room with him. This was insane and inhumane. I FREAKED OUT. The last thing I remember hearing was someone on the medical team whispering through their mask, "We need to go get her parents."

CHAPTER 7

Behind the Glass

I don't remember my parents walking through the door. I don't remember what I said to them. Apparently, I had blacked out. Trauma and shock have a way of doing that. However, what they told me is this... they walked through the door, and I was completely distraught. They hadn't been provided an update on Colby or his condition by the hospital worker that had brought them to the room, and I could barely speak to tell them. I was crying, shaking, and all I could get out of my mouth was "It is not good." Eventually, one of the doctors came and explained to my parents what they had just told me. My Mom, being a former nurse, asked a few questions. One of them being, are his pupils reactive? And with the doctor's answer and her sober eye contact, my parents then knew too, this wasn't going to end well.

Some of the worries of my parents and Colby's medical team quickly shifted on me when my body went into shock. I became extremely weak and was on the verge of fainting. Someone brought me apple juice in one of those pre-packaged cups. I refused to drink it. After a while, my Dad and one of the nurses eventually compromised with me and asked me if I would eat a slice of banana bread from the hospital coffee shop. I said "yes" so, my Dad went to get me one but I never ate it. I didn't care to eat or drink ever again. I remember feeling like it wasn't just Colby dying, I was dying too. I felt like my body was shutting down and here they were asking what I wanted to eat or drink. I understand they were worried about me. I understand they told me I needed to eat and be strong so I could be there for Colby. However, how did they expect me to do anything in the world minutes after they told me I couldn't see my dying husband? "Let me starve. Let me die with him. I don't give two craps about eating or drinking anything right now. I wanted it to be my brain instead. I wanted it to be me. I should die over Colby. If Colby doesn't make it, neither do I. If Colby dies, I go with him. Were brain transplants a thing? I would give him mine. I am not sticking around and have no interest in surviving this shattering pain without him. I am not willing to survive this." These were the things going on in my mind as people were asking me to take a sip of apple juice. I hate apple juice- I will for the rest of my life.

People always talk about the mental and emotional impact of trauma and grief but never the physical impact. The physical impact began that day and for months after Colby died, it would almost kill me too.

I remember my Dad having to leave a few minutes later to head to the airport. The Oilers had gotten Colby's parents, sister, and her boyfriend a flight to Toronto from Saskatchewan. While we were waiting for them to arrive, I asked my Mom if she could help me to the bathroom. I could barely walk but I wanted to try so she held me as I shuffled my way down the hall. When we started our way back from the bathroom, I saw Colby... kinda. Colby was coming back from a scan and there were a handful of nurses and doctors slowly wheeling him back into the unit. He was covered in tubes and wires. My adrenaline kicked in and I started to run toward him with everything I had in me. I just wanted to hold his hand in the hallway as they pushed him back into the unit. But they stopped dead in their tracks. They looked at my Mom and they looked at me. The next thing I know, I was being pushed back into the waiting room against my own will. I watched Colby's bed roll past me through the window on the door. There are so many words I could use to describe the way I felt being kept from Colby, not just at that moment, but in his final four days… the most graceful one… without swearing… would be completely inhumane.

All we could do was wait. While waiting, I started returning calls. The NHL, the Bruins, the Oilers, family, friends, etc. I was also informed by the medical team that the media, fans, and other random people were already calling and pretending to be me to get information. Colby was just out of surgery and the world wanted an update and was willing to do whatever to get it. Imagine that for a minute. Sitting there in this tiny room, just learning the worst news possible, and then on top of everything happening we were going to have to make my husband unidentified because people were treating us like we were the "next big news story". It was and still is absolutely disgusting. In the end, myself, and one of the NHL doctors would be given a designated password to use when we called to get information on Colby - the password was lime green. I don't remember why or how I picked that color. I want to say it was because of the color of the magazine on one of the coffee tables in the waiting room, but I can't remember for sure.

My phone was blowing up and I was incredibly overwhelmed so I shifted my focus on only updating a handful of people who could then pass the information down the line. My Mom and Dad were providing updates to the rest. I was in over my head. Overwhelmed and in shock would be an understatement.

A few minutes later the door opened and one of the critical care nurses walked in with a wheelchair. We had come up with a plan that would allow me to see Colby from behind the glass of his critical care room window. It was the best plan we could come up with and it had to be super quick. One nurse would go into his room with one walkie-talkie and the other nurse would stand outside with me with the other walkie-talkie. I remember being wheeled to his room as the other nurses and doctors stared at us. When I arrived outside Colby's room, he looked completely different than when I had seen him earlier that morning. His cheeks were back to his rosy cheek color compared to the white and hypothermic state I had seen him in that morning. Honestly, it just looked like he was sleeping with a lot of tubes and wires attached to him. He had a wrap around his head from his surgery. But other than that, he honestly looked peaceful. I watched the nurse tie his wedding band to his ankle with a piece of string. Then the conversation began. It would be one of the last that I would have with my husband. As the whole critical care unit watched. I sobbed through the walkie-talkie and told Colby he had to wake up. He couldn't die on me. He wasn't allowed to leave me. I told him how much I loved him and how much I needed him. How much we all needed him. I told him "You have to wake up." I feel like I probably said that a million times. Then I asked the nurse to squeeze his hand three times.

Three hand squeezes... they were Colby's and my thing. Three hand squeezes means I love you. We started this very early on in our relationship. He would squeeze my hand in the car. I would squeeze his hand in the grocery store. We would do it anywhere and everywhere. Every night before bed we would fall asleep holding hands. We would always say goodnight and then do our three hand squeezes. It took everything in me to not break through that window and go hold his hand myself. The thought of Colby dying alone was destroying me. Despite it being out of my control, I will never forgive myself for it. It haunts me to this day. Three hand squeezes through a critical care nurse were the only way I could tell him that I loved him and that I always will. I pray every day somehow the nurse squeezing his hand as we had always done, Colby felt I was right there beside him. But the guilt I carry will never go away.

After my walkie-talkie conversation with Colby, I was rolled back to the waiting room to wait for Colby's family. They would eventually arrive, and the team let us go back to see Colby once again through the window. They also talked briefly through the walkie-talkie.

Then the time came... one of the hardest things I have ever had to do. The staff informed us we'd have to go home for the night and they would inform us if anything drastically changed. I begged the doctor one more time to lock me in his room. I told them I promised I wouldn't leave the room if they'd just let me in. I just wanted to be with him. I just didn't want him to be alone. They didn't budge on their decision. We could tell they weren't going to change their minds. So, they sent us home. They just told us to go home and wait...

CHAPTER 8

Those 4 Days

The waiting game. Pure agony and torture. Not being able to be there to hold Colb's hand. Knowing my 25-year-old husband was dying alone. Knowing there was nothing I could do about it. I've never felt so helpless in my entire life. I begged. I pleaded. I told the hospital staff I'd literally give anything to be in the room with him. The guilt I still carry for not trying harder. For not doing more. I will never forgive myself. But I also know there was nothing I could have said or done to change the situation. Covid restrictions robbed me. Inhumane is an understatement.

I didn't sleep much but when I woke up Wednesday morning, I realized it was the first morning in a very long time Colb wasn't by my side or I didn't wake up to a good morning text because he was on the road. Colb was in a coma, and I wondered if I'd ever get to wake up next to him again. Easter weekend was just around the corner. Good Friday was three days away. I posted this on my Instagram while waiting at home, asking for everyone to pray for Colby to be an Easter miracle.

"I'm waiting for you, Colb. I always make you wait so now it is my turn to wait for you. I made you wait years before going out on a date with you. I made you wait at the altar. I make you wait every day when I'm rushing to get ready. I make you wait until I decide what I want to eat. Chester makes you wait until he wants to pee in crappy weather or play fetch late hours of the night. The list could go on. You always wait for us, so now we're waiting for you. However long it takes, I'm waiting for you. You can do it; you can be a miracle. You need to be a miracle. I know you can. I'm so proud to be your wife, Colby Cave. I love you so much. I always will."

On the same day, our friends, Kelly and David Backes (former Bruins' teammate), would start an NHL prayer call. Players, coaches, and their families from all over the world would join a zoom link and pray for Colby to wake up. Everyone seemed so hopeful. I listened to the zoom but could barely speak. So many hockey people rallied around Colb and me. This really did show how powerful the entire hockey family was.

The hospital dietician called me mid-morning to ask if he had any food allergies? I was surprised by the question considering they were just feeding him through a tube. I was surprised by so many things happening and because of Covid, the wires, the tubes, the procedures, and all the bandages were never really explained to me. I feel if I had been there in person, I would have been able to get clarity on so many things. But I was only allowed to see Colby for a few minutes on FaceTime. That was it. Wires everywhere. His eyes were glued shut. His head was half shaved. Tubes all over. I remember thinking the IV in his arm didn't look comfortable. It bothered me so much. I was fixated on it. So much that I would eventually get a tattoo of our wedding date on the exact arm, where the IV was. I'm sure the IV was right where it was supposed to be, it just looked so out of place on FaceTime. Everything looked out of place. Nothing about it looked right.

I was told hearing is the last thing to go and was so grateful for the nurses willing to bring an iPad into Colb's room so I could talk to him. The two chances I got to FaceTime him, I would tell him that he needed to wake up. I would tell him how much I love him. And I would tell him I'd be willing to wait forever and a day for him to come back to me. I felt like I was watching my husband die through a phone screen. I don't have the words to describe the pain. The helplessness. I wanted to jump through the screen. I wanted to break into the critical care unit. The anger I felt for these rules can never be described in words.

After that morning's FaceTime ended, we came up with the idea to start collecting "wakeup" videos for Colby from family, friends, and teammates to put on his iPad so they could play them repeatedly in his room. I asked the staff if they would be willing to do that for us if we dropped off his iPad. I was so happy they agreed to do this for us. I wanted to make sure even though he couldn't have us physically there, he could hear and feel we were still cheering him on like crazy. Colby never got to hear these videos. However, I still have the PowerPoint on his iPad. The PowerPoint is called "Caver Strong." Sometimes I have the strength to listen to them. Other times, it is just too hard and brings me right back to those four days.

My sister, Ky decided to book a flight for the next day (Thursday) to fly in. My brother-in-law, Dave, and niece Sydnie would stay behind in BC until we knew more because of the strict travel restrictions.

The flowers and meals started to arrive from all over the world. I felt like all this stuff was happening around me and everything was spinning so fast, and everyone wasn't just waiting for Colb to wake up, but also waiting to see how I was going to react to it all. I could barely eat. I actually refused to. Again, how could I eat at a time like this? Wednesday was just a blur. The waiting game blur. But then came Thursday. Thursday it became even more real that Colby was dying. There was nothing else they could do and today may be his last day.

I got a call from the head of critical care that Colby had taken a turn for the worse and he may only have a few hours left. Maybe a day if we were lucky. I would once again BEG the doctor to let me come and be there as he took his last breaths. I fought with everything in my power. I made all the important calls to try to get me into that hospital. So did the NHL. They rallied around me. We called the ethics committee of the hospital. We tried every single thing we could. However, we all got the same answer- no.

I am normally not an angry person, and it takes a lot to really set me off but when that doctor told me I couldn't be there as Colby was taking his last breaths, I lost it. I yelled at him. I told him he was killing my husband. I told him he was a horrible person for not letting me be there. I was shaking. I was furious. I said so many mean things to him. I've never in my life been so angry. All I wanted was to be with my husband as he took his last breaths. As strange as this is to even write, I just wanted to be next to my husband when he died. And I wasn't allowed to be. I still have no idea what Colby's last moments and breaths were like, and it haunts me to this day.

I knew my sister was about to leave for the airport when I ended the call with the doctor. As soon as we hung up, I called her but couldn't even get any words out. I was hysterical. All she heard was "It is not good. You all need to come now." She hung up and within ten minutes a taxi was not just picking her up but now my brother-in-law and my niece too. They just dropped what they were doing, threw everything into a bag, and rushed to the airport.

I started calling some of our best friends, teammates, and coaches. I told them that Colby only had a few hours left. Some cried. Some stared blankly back at me speechless. Some continued to tell me that he was a fighter and that he wasn't going to die. After all those calls, I did what everyone advised me not to do. I drove an hour to the hospital and stormed my way up to the critical care unit. I refused to accept no as an answer. Because of my determination, I unexpectedly was given a few minutes to see him. A few minutes meaning maybe 10 whole minutes. It was even more painful leaving after that because I knew he was dying, and I couldn't stay. It was just a matter of time until he died. And he was going to die alone.

My sister and her family arrived Thursday evening. I vaguely remember walking upstairs to meet her as she came through the door. She would tell me later that all I could get out of my mouth was, "I need to know if he's going to live." My sister slept with me that night and every night, for the next four weeks. I slept on Colby's side. She slept on mine. When asking her about some of her memories for this book, she shared with me, "So many nights, when you would finally fall asleep, I heard you whimpering in your sleep, it was heartbreaking".

Friday. Colby made it through the night. That morning I got a call from the doctor, and he asked me for permission to do a scan. They needed to see if something else was going on in his brain. He also told me there was a high risk involved with this scan. If they lowered him in the slightest way, the pressure on his brain would rise and he could code. We didn't know if he would make it out of the scan, but the doctor urged me it was something he really thought they should do. I trusted him and I gave him my approval.

The scan was supposed to start around 11:30 am. There was a scheduled NHL prayer call at 11:00 am. I told my friends leading the call if I hung up in the middle of the prayer call, it was because the doctors were calling me and there was a chance Colby didn't make it. At the same time, I still wanted everyone to pray for a miracle. One of the Bruins' wives recorded the call that day. She told me she wanted to send it to me so when Colby woke up, he would see how many people were praying for him and how loved he was. A few months later, I listened to this prayer call. I listened to myself completely broken, begging everyone to "Just pray that he wakes up." Pleading with them all, "He has to wake up." To be honest, it doesn't even sound like me, I felt like I was listening to someone else.

It took hours before we learned if Colby made it through his scan. There were many moments when I thought I would be getting the call that he didn't. Finally, after a few hours, I heard that he made it through, and they said we could FaceTime him. It turned out that this FaceTime would be the last time he would hear our voices. As I did with each Facetime; I told him how much I love him. I told him how much I still need him. I told him that he couldn't die. He wasn't allowed to die. I didn't want to hang up the call. I wanted to tell him so much more. But the call ended and that was it. It was the last time he heard my voice.

I asked my parents to call one of our best family friends- Jack Vos. He married Colby and me. He also was a widower until he remarried my Mom's best friend who was also a widow- Deb Vanluesen. If you recall at the beginning of the book when we had the caravan back to my parents when we landed, we used their car. Jack is the closest person I have ever had to a grandparent. We have a special bond. I asked my parents to call him so he could come over and pray with me. Jack is in his mid-80s. When he walked through the door, he sat right beside me as I laid on the floor sobbing. He just began to pray for me. For us.

He talked about how I might need to let Colb go and if he passed he would no longer be in pain. He would be healed. And he would be heading to the best place he could ever be. Jack talked about Heaven and what that's going to be like. His presence that day meant so much to me and my family.

Still to this day, Jack gets emotional thinking about that day. He says he has never met a more perfect couple for each other. He said out of all the deaths he has experienced in his lifetime, Colby's death is so senseless and hard to understand. Many people asked me after Colby died, how I still have faith. I think it is because of my Christian family, friends, and pastors like Jack. They let me be angry. They let me swear. They let me cry. They didn't force religion down my throat. They let me feel every emotion I felt. Also that same day, I had a phone call with one of our church friends- Donnie. Donnie let me be angry and honestly, it was the best thing for me. So here is a gentle reminder for us all. Don't force religion or beliefs on anyone in times like this. You can pray. You can support them. But, before you tell someone in immense pain and grief to be grateful for what they have had and everything happens for a reason, think about which one of your loved ones you're willing to give up right now.

The day turned to night and Colby was still alive. Every second mattered at this point. I remember talking on FaceTime with my sister to one of our close friends who graduated from Harvard Med. It was around 1:00 am and I couldn't sleep. He was trying to explain to me the medical terms, the wires in the pictures that they would send me of Colby on life support and talk me through what was going on in Colby's brain.

The rarity of a colloid cyst and dying of one is something that makes me sick to my stomach. I often think back, what did I miss? How could I have saved him? A few days later, an article was published by the head neurologist in Canada saying that "Colby Cave's death is a result of very, very bad luck."

That night I laid in our bed beside my sister knowing my husband, my best friend probably wasn't going to make it through the night. I was over an hour away from the hospital, and the love of my life was dying alone. I was just waiting for a call that would tell me his heart had officially stopped.

CHAPTER 9

April 11, 2020

I woke up to my Mom running down the basement stairs, about two hours after I eventually fell asleep. As soon as she walked through the door she blurted out, "He is gone. Colby is gone." I woke up completely caught off guard. For some reason, I missed 11 calls from the hospital even though my phone was on loud. We got the call just after 3:00 am that Colby's heart had stopped. At that moment I felt like my heart stopped too. I'm not sure it has beat the same since my Mom woke me up with those words that morning. I wasn't there to hold his hand. I wasn't there when he took his last breath. This haunts me every second of the day. My words will always fall short trying to describe how much I miss him. I just know now that our reunion in Heaven will be the greatest one ever.

After I gained my composure, I called the doctor back. He told me that Colby's blood pressure just kept dropping, he was already three times sedated, and there was nothing they could have done. I told him how amazing Colby was. How loved he was. How he didn't get the chance to hear all the wake-up videos. He told me I was allowed to come to the hospital to say goodbye to his body. I asked about organ donation and for his brain for research but was told they would not take them because of Covid.

I hung up and started making calls, before getting dressed and driving to the hospital. The first call I made was to Colby's billet parents, Kim and Brian. They knew right away when they saw my number on the phone. We talked for a few minutes, and I learned later that as soon as they got off the phone they made a grilled cheese sandwich, despite it being the middle of the night. It was Colby's staple meal at their house for so many years. The next calls I made were to Colby's coaches. Neither of them picked up. Then I called his agent. I had put some of his best friends in a group chat and just texted them, "He is dead." Looking back, it is amazing to me what your body and mind do when it is in shock. I was so worried and focused on Colby's other loved ones hearing it from me, I didn't really process what I was telling them. I couldn't process it. Colby was alive and fine on Monday, and now Saturday, he was gone. He was never coming back.

After countless hugs and so many tears, it took all the strength I had left in me to get dressed. I put on one of Colb's favorite sweaters. I put on his deodorant (something that I started wearing the day he was helicoptered away and still do to this day). I got into the car, and we drove for an hour in complete silence. No one prepared me for what I was about to see and go through. How could this be happening to me?

By the time we arrived at the hospital, Colby had been gone for a few hours. They were waiting to take his body to the morgue until I got there to see him. It still confuses me how I was allowed to see him after he died but couldn't be there when he was dying. I'll never understand that. But in the moment I was grateful I was allowed to see his body. As we approached the front doors, I got into an argument with one of the security workers. I told him I had to go up to the critical care unit to see my husband who just passed away. He just kept saying he wouldn't let me pass until I told him who my husband was. The problem was I couldn't tell him because Colby was unidentified, and we hadn't released to the public he had died. Heck, I still hadn't even seen him, and it was in the early hours of the morning. We would argue back and forth, all while I was trying to call the critical care doctor to come down and let us up. I eventually got so annoyed with the guy I just decided to run right past him to the elevator. No one was stopping me from seeing my husband and he was in my way.

When we arrived at the unit, the head of critical care was there waiting for me and Colby's parents and sister. We were also greeted by the nurse who was there on Tuesday when Colby went to surgery. The same nurse who I would tell to squeeze Colby's hand three times. She told me she remembered what that meant, and as Colby was dying and took his last breaths, she squeezed his hand three times for me. It brought me a small amount of comfort, but nothing could prepare me for walking into the room and seeing Colby. They encouraged us to gown, mask, and glove up in order to go and see him. But I refused. There was no chance I was holding my husband's hand and body for the last time in gloves or kissing him goodbye through a mask. The image of walking into the room and seeing Colby in that bed, still gives me nightmares. His coloring was so off. He was so yellow. He was so cold. He was stiff. Your body starts to secrete fluids and it was coming out of his nose. The smell was awful. A smell I can still remember. None of it mattered. I crawled on top of him right away. I just laid on top of his cold body. Gut-wrenching doesn't even begin to describe what it was like laying on his chest and not hearing or feeling his heartbeat.

I knew this was the very last time I could lay on him. Kiss him. Touch him. Hold his hand. We cut a piece of his hair. The same color as mine, and the same color we prayed for our ginger babies to have one day. We took his wedding ring off his finger and the one attached to his ankle. I could have laid there forever with him. I never wanted to get off his body. The amount of physical, mental, and emotional pain of never being able to see, touch, or hold him again, was unbearable and it still is today. Colby was the best thing to ever happen to me. He was my person. My hero. Crying over the body of the person you love most in your life traumatizes you. And now, here I was, a widow, before our first wedding anniversary. I thought maybe if I just laid on top of him, I could warm up his body, and he would wake up. I didn't want to get off because I knew my walking out of that room would be the last time I ever saw him. I don't know how long I was there. Could have been minutes, could have been hours. But eventually, I was told that I had to leave. I remember it taking every cell in my body to peel myself off of him. To kiss him one last time. And to walk out of the door. On my way out of his room, the nurse handed me a Ziploc bag of his clothes that he last wore. Those clothes are still in the same Ziploc bag. I have yet to open them.

We walked out of the hospital, got back into the car, and drove an hour back home. Every ounce of me hated that building. It was the building where my husband died alone. Some days, I think I should go back. Some days, I think I never could. I still have so much anger and hurt. I think I always will. I have learned the reality is, not everyone dies peacefully surrounded by family and friends. Sometimes death is tragic and awful. Grief is not only accepting our loved one has died but a search for peace over how they died. I am still working on this. I wasn't home long before the word started spreading. I was asked to make a public statement about Colby's passing for the NHL to post before it was leaked by someone else.

"It is with great sadness to share the news that our Colby Cave passed away this morning. Both our families are in shock but know our Colby was loved dearly by us, his family and friends, the entire hockey community, and many more. We thank everyone for their prayers during this difficult time."

The number of calls and messages I began to receive was overwhelming. Barrie, ON, where my parents live, sold out of flowers. The whole city sold out of flowers. They were sent by every NHL team, every AHL team, referees, friends, teammates, and family. We had over 80 bouquets delivered. All this stuff was happening all around me and I had no idea how to process it all. I just sobbed. That's all I could do. I told everyone that I just wish it would have been me. I would have done anything for it to be me instead of Colb. For better or for worse, in sickness and health, I would have done everything in my power to keep Colb alive. I felt like a failure. I heard so many coaches, teammates, and friends, cry back through the phone and tell me how much Colby loved and still loves me. How Chester and I were his everything, and his #1 forever. Normally, friends and family would come over instantly when you lose someone. However, none of our family and friends could come over because of Covid restrictions. So instead, they would send their condolences through the phone, through flowers, meals, and text messages. It would be weeks before I got my first physical hug from some of our friends. Another completely messed up thing due to Covid restrictions.

I remember dinner that night. Everyone went to sit around the table. I was shocked that food was even a thing right now. I couldn't process taking one bite. And every single person had their person to sit beside. But I didn't. There was one empty chair. I didn't have my person next to me anymore. I was so upset everyone else had their person and mine was gone. Some people were drinking, and some were eating. Meanwhile, I felt like a zombie. How could anyone think about eating or drinking or even talking at this point? I could barely breathe. This was so unfair. The pain was all-consuming. People kept telling me how strong I was and how brave I was, but the truth was my life had lost all meaning in a split second. Because Colb was my world, my whole world, and now my world was gone.

He filled my life with so much joy and love. He completed me and made me who I was. I saw my life in him. And now he was gone. My person was gone.

That night, people from all over the world put their hockey sticks out by their front doors for Colby. Thousands of strangers, family, and friends wanted to do this as a beautiful tribute to Colby. To show their love and support in the best way they could. I don't think I ever really grasped how amazing this gesture was for people to do. I couldn't. There is a picture taken of Chester and me outside the front door with Colb's stick. I look like a complete shell of myself. I had no idea what was ahead of me. I was 26, I was now a widow.

April 11, 2020 will always go down as the worst day of my life. A nightmare that I just can't seem to wake up from. I was supposed to spend the rest of my life with Colb. But that day, I realized that though Colb spent the rest of his life with me, I'd have to spend the rest of mine without him. I will always be honored I was the one he loved till the day he died. I went to bed that night and the only thing keeping me alive was knowing when I woke up, I was one day closer to seeing him in Heaven. I now had a sweet angel hubby waiting up there for me and I longed for the day to meet him with a warm wet kiss. I was hoping it was going to be sooner than later. But for now, I just knew I had the best guardian angel anyone could ever have.

CHAPTER 10

The First 48 Hours

"The death of a spouse or partner is different than other losses because it literally changes every single thing in your world going forward. When your spouse dies even the way you eat changes. The way you watch TV changes. Your friend circle changes (or disappears entirely). Your family dynamic/ life changes (or disappears entirely). Your financial status changes. Your job situation changes. It affects your self-worth. Your self-esteem. Your confidence. Your rhythms. The way you breathe. Your mentality. Your brain functions. Ever heard the term 'widow brain?' If you don't know what that is, count yourself very lucky. Your physical body. Your hobbies and interests. Your sense of security. Your sense of humor. Your sense of womanhood or manhood. EVERY. SINGLE. THING. CHANGES. You are handed a new life that you never asked for and that you don't particularly want. It is the hardest, most gut-wrenching, horrific, life-altering thing to live with."

- Kelley Lynn

This quote was sent to me from an Instagram follower.

The average age of a widow is 59 years old. I became one at

26 years old, just two weeks shy of my 27th birthday. I woke up on Easter Sunday as a widow. I still can't wrap my head around the fact that I became a widow before our first wedding anniversary. When you marry someone, they say "two people become one." I knew Colb better than anyone else in this world. And he knew the same for me. That's what marriage is all about. It's about knowing every inch of your spouse like the back of your own hand.

The rarity of his death caused by a colloid cyst still upsets me to this day. He was perfectly fine and what seemed to be perfectly healthy until he wasn't. And then, just like that, he was gone. Looking back on it now, there is something unique about being so connected to your spouse, physically, emotionally, mentally, and spiritually. My gut was right those weeks before he died knowing something wasn't good. Even though my gut "knew it," my heart could have never been prepared for this magnitude of trauma, pain, and loss. Colb wasn't coming back. Less than a year earlier we had just picked out our wedding rings, suits, dresses, and flowers. And now, I realized I'd have to pick out a funeral home to be in charge of Colby's dead body.

The day prior (the day Colb died), my Dad started looking up funeral homes in Barrie. Something, I couldn't even think about doing at the time. However, the following morning, I knew I needed to start making decisions. He told me about the two funeral homes he thought would be best and I picked one of them. My Dad called the hospital and arranged for Colb's body to be sent there. Looking back, there were many times like this when my parents didn't get an opportunity to grieve properly because they were doing all the things I couldn't handle. The "business side" of death is something you don't realize is even a thing, until it becomes a thing. I'm just so grateful for them and all they did for me. The way they stepped up when I couldn't was incredible and I'm not sure how I'd have done any of it without them.

That afternoon Colby's agent called me to say that the Oilers and Bruins wanted to start a memorial fund in his honor. They allowed me to make all the decisions of what the memorial fund would support. Ultimately, the final decision ended up being two things. Proceeds from the fund would go towards:

1. Community programs with an emphasis on mental health initiatives.
2. Providing access to sports for underprivileged children.

I made a statement about the memorial fund and had no idea of the impact it was going to have on not just my life, but so many other people's lives too.

"My greatest honor in life will always be that I am Colby Cave's wife. I love him dearly, I always will, and miss him beyond words. He taught me so much. He was genuine, caring, selfless, and had a contagious laughter, but most importantly had the biggest heart. Though our time with him on earth was cut short, I am grateful that the whole world can now see how incredible my husband was and how lucky I am to be his wife. Colby would be humbled by the Colby Cave Memorial Fund, and I am looking forward to continuing his legacy alongside the Edmonton Oilers and the rest of the hockey community."

As Wendy Tippett said to the media, "When a wife or a fiancé passes away, the whole team is still there for that person. When it's the husband that's gone, that's the connection to the team. Often the wife is left alone. I just don't want that to happen to her. Everyone has taken that directly to heart."

Our hockey family completely wrapped their arms around me and helped me stay afloat from the very first day. They continue to do so today. The memorial fund was one of the greatest things that the NHL family could have given to me. It gave me a purpose to get out of bed each morning. The memorial fund is one of the ways that I get to try to fulfill the nickname Colb gave me. His little world changer. I had no idea the memorial fund would make such a huge impact helping others. It has surpassed my expectations.

My phone wouldn't stop blowing up. The news of Colb's death had spread all over the world. My Instagram was blowing up. The followers, notifications, the DMs, the news articles. I was completely in over my head, and everyone was watching me. I was drowning. I was numb. All I wanted was Colby back. He would have handled this all so much better. I wasn't used to this. I sure didn't ask for any of it.

"Emily Cave hit the international spotlight following the death of NHL superstar Colby Cave- her husband. Up until the passing, she stepped in the limelight by continuously providing updates on Colby's status." - Stars Offline

All the flowers and meals and gifts were all beautiful but also overwhelming at the same time. I don't think that I was in a place to really process everything that was happening around me. Once again, I cannot stress enough about deaths during Covid, your family and friends can't come over right away to comfort you like they normally would have. You aren't able to hug your support system, share stories, laugh, and cry together. We were all robbed of that. Our best friends would only be able to support me through a screen. It would be weeks before I would be able to hug someone that wasn't my immediate family. It was isolating. It was lonely. It was horrific. So, flowers, meals, and gifts were the only way people could show their love and support. It broke so many of our friend's hearts, not being able to be there. They lost Colby too, and we couldn't be together. I just wanted all the pain to end. My body ached. This was supposed to be our first Easter together as a married couple. We were supposed to have ginger little babies to do Easter egg hunts with for so many years to come. Nothing made sense anymore.

Colby's family told me they were leaving the next day. They wanted to get back to their family, friends, and farm. His sister and some of their family friends planned a parade to greet them as they drove back into North Battleford. There was a planned get-together with all their closest people at the farm.

The first 24-36 hours without Colb seems like a complete blur. However, looking back, there were so many decisions made during those hours I can't even believe I had to make. It is crazy to me how much work needs to be done when a loved one dies. And you're making these decisions while still in complete shock. Again, without my parents, I wouldn't have been able to do it all.

The next morning, 48 hours after Colby died, his family left. The parade the town had for them was a beautiful gesture by so many people. It was also incredibly hard for me because, while the parade was happening, I was standing in the funeral home with my parents, making all these decisions while still in shock. Many of those in attendance at the parade may have thought they were "bringing Colby back to North Battleford" during the parade. The truth was that wasn't even close to what was happening. Colby's body would go in a body bag from the hospital to the funeral home, but from the funeral home to the crematory, he would be put in a cardboard box "casket" unless I picked out a wooden casket for him. A ten-minute drive to the crematory. Can you imagine? It was painful knowing that there is a massive support system and parade going on in another province, and I am sitting in a funeral home with my parents, picking out a casket for Colb, because I couldn't stand the thought of him being thrown into a cardboard box to drive even 10 minutes in.

How was it he was alive less than a week ago? Now here I am, begging the funeral home director to let me see his body one more time. I just wanted to kiss him again one more time. I just wanted to touch him one more time. I honestly thought about just sprinting through every room until I found his body bag. I also wanted that for my parents. They had witnessed him being taken away in the ambulance from their house and then helicoptered off, but they never saw him again after that. We were told no again and again because of Covid.

Here's the thing, I knew Colby wanted to be cremated because we had talked about it during those weeks while watching Grey's Anatomy. I respected every wish I knew he wanted. However, my parents and I had never dealt with cremation before. The funeral director told my Dad before our arrival, to bring some of Colby's favorite things. So, I brought a wedding picture of us, his rubber wedding ring that he worked out in, and Chester's blanket. I remember waking up in the middle of the night, months later, feeling so guilty I never thought to cremate him in his favorite outfit. After picking out his casket, the funeral director sent me home with a catalog of pictures of urns. He would also take his fingerprints so all of our family members could order a fingerprint necklace if we chose to. There were so many decisions to be made. It literally makes me sick to my stomach to think about what I was going through that day. I am forever grateful for my parents being there, and to my sister and brother-in-law for staying for four weeks to help me with all of this. We knew we wouldn't be able to have a funeral for a while because of Covid. But I would have never expected how long it would take for us to eventually have one. Even when we finally could have his celebration of life, there would still be many restrictions. To be honest, there were many times that I thought maybe I'd just die soon, and we could just have a double funeral together.

I walked out of the funeral home that afternoon not even comprehending all I had just done. I just picked out a casket. I just gave a funeral director a picture from our wedding, and Chester's blanket, for my 25-year-old husband to be cremated in. I went home and started googling the process. How cremation works. What does a crematory even look like? This was all so new to me. Covid made it hard for things to be done and explained appropriately.

That night, Colby's family would have people over at their farm. His cousin sent me a video without others knowing of everyone together. All I saw was people drinking, laughing, crying, and celebrating Colby's life without me. It was painfully hard to see all that happening as I was sitting on the couch going through a catalog of urns, trying to find one Colby would love and would suit him perfectly. I eventually found it. And then I just sobbed. The next morning, 72 hours after he passed, his body was scheduled to be cremated. And I had just picked the urn that would hold his remains. I still just couldn't believe this was all happening.

Life is made up of moments, good and bad, big and small. It was at that moment I knew my life was never going to be the same. Colby and I had gone through hard times, but we had each other to go through them with. You don't get over something like this. I remember praying I would just die too. I didn't want to have to be strong. I didn't want to have to make these decisions. I wanted my old life back. I just wanted to be normal. I just wanted to be with Colb again. I just wanted to die. The idea of dying and being with Colby again was the only thing that would comfort me.

CHAPTER 11

Widow

For the past two and half years, there have been many days where I've wondered, what would it have felt like to be a normal twenty something year old. And to be completely honest, there have been so many times that I have cried wishing my life could just be "normal."

Colby hadn't even been gone for a week before I got my period. I know that probably doesn't even seem like something I should share but you must realize the emotional anguish that came with that. It reminded me I will never have a child with Colby. I realized he and I will never use the list of baby names I had on my phone. I had not only lost the love of my life, but I also would never bear his child. I changed my phone list into a list of "death duties" because I couldn't stand looking at the names that we had picked out. I felt robbed

Like most young newlyweds, Colby and I didn't have a will. Why would we? We were too young to even think about doing something like that. We were only thinking of life together, not death. I don't even think having a will ever crossed our minds. Which turned out to be a massive mistake, only making life so much more complicated than it should be. Having no will is something I am still dealing with, nearly three years later. So please, I beg you, if you are reading this and don't have a will, stop reading. Go make it happen. If you have one and it hasn't been updated in a while, stop what you're doing and go update it. It's just something you don't want to ever have to deal with. Another piece of advice since we are discussing the "business" side of death, make sure to write down all your passwords somewhere safe and let your person know where they are. I didn't know any of Colby's passwords and trying to get access to his accounts has been difficult. There are a hundred more examples of why these things need to be done. Trust me on this, take the time to do it now.

My phone never stopped blowing up. People from all over the world seemed to be rallying around us. One of those people who reached out was Carli Skaggs. She was a young widow and could really relate as well. Her husband Tyler played baseball and also passed away before their first wedding anniversary. She would become my go-to girl. She was in the public eye too. She got it. She understood what I was dealing with. She was the first "widow friend" that I made. It's a club that I never imagined being a part of but at the same time, I am so grateful for every person in it. They get it. They get me. They never stop showing up. Some of my best friends now are widows and widowers. We are all brought together by a tragedy. No one can take that bond away from us. It makes me wonder at times if all our spouses are in Heaven together supporting and encouraging each other, just like we are down here.

I know finding a great therapist isn't the easiest thing in the world. I know admitting you need one isn't either. I was encouraged to find a therapist right away. I want to believe Colb was watching out for me as I was fortunate enough to be referred to an amazing therapist on day one of becoming a widow. In the beginning, I talked to her almost every single day on FaceTime. I'm certain I would not be where I am today without her continual guidance and support. Therapy is one of the things that has completely changed my life. I will always be an advocate that therapy is a valuable thing. Thank you will never be enough for my therapist for all she has done and the way she has helped me through the darkest time of my life. Having that person who I can fully trust to be a sounding board and provide unbiased advice was and still is needed in many situations I went through and continue to go through.

Looking back on the first week, many kind gestures were displayed to myself and my family. One was a drive-by in front of my parent's house. It was organized by friends and colleagues showing their support as they knew and felt bad, I had missed the one held in Saskatchewan. I remember having trouble even standing up, let alone standing outside as people slowed down in their cars with signs of encouragement and support. Before the drive-by started, one of Colby's teammates and his wife came over and stood in the driveway. We met them during our time in Bakersfield- Anthony and Courtney Peluso. Although I couldn't hug them, it brought so much comfort knowing such good friends lived right down the street. I will never forget walking out of the front door and seeing them standing there. I wanted to run and give them the biggest hugs. They were our people. I immediately made eye contact with Anthony, he had to turn away almost immediately, as he could not control his own painful emotions. It took everything in him to try and hold it together for me. This wasn't just one of Colby's many teammates. This was one of his brothers. It still pains me so much that we had to stand 6 feet apart during this time. We couldn't hug our people. I'll never take another hug for granted.

The news of an NHL player fighting for his life and then his tragic death four days later spread quickly worldwide. Reporters calling, texting, emailing asking for statements, drones flying over the house, and cameras outside the front door all contributed to me refusing to go any further than our front porch. Our front porch was literally the only meeting place I could say hi to friends that would stop by and stand on the front lawn. It was so difficult to see friends who loved Colby and felt my pain and yet not physically be allowed to embrace them. Each time I saw someone, I'd break down crying. Each time, I felt my whole being getting weaker. The first 15 days after losing Colb, it took all I had in me to put on a brave face and simply survive another day. I felt like a zombie. I felt so alone. I didn't shower for days. I didn't see the point. I lost all motivation to do anything. I was at the lowest of lows when I received a DM from a follower that sent me completely over the edge. This follower told me that she was there the night that Colby died. She knew his exact room number. Her boyfriend was in the critical care unit too, and every night she could go in and see him at 11:00 pm. She was sharing this all with me because I was giving her the motivation to keep going if her boyfriend didn't make it. At the time I didn't take it that way and I immediately FREAKED out.

She was there the night Colby died but I wasn't allowed to be? She was able to be with her boyfriend, and I wasn't allowed to be with my husband. I remember thinking, what am I even hearing right now? I started screaming. I called the critical care unit and lost it on the doctor on duty that night. I asked him how it was possible that a girlfriend was allowed to see her boyfriend, but I wasn't allowed to be with my husband. He didn't know too much about it and legally, he wasn't allowed to say much. I was so ANGRY and couldn't fathom what I was learning.

The next morning, I received a call from Colby's doctor, who also happened to be the head of critical care. He explained to me a rule had been put in place that if you were 24 or younger, they considered you a child. Covid, or not, because you were considered a child at 24, family and friends could come in and be with you if you were dying. Colby had just turned 25 less than 4 months prior, but they weren't willing to make an exception for him. I just couldn't even believe any of this was happening.

Along with all the pain and anger I felt for not being able to be with Colby, I was also just days away from having to face one of the many "firsts" that come during the first year of widowhood. My 27th birthday was just around the corner, I dreaded it. I didn't want to celebrate life while I was dealing with death. How could I celebrate without Colby? It was supposed to be my first one as Colb's wife, not his widow. There was nothing happy about my birthday. I didn't want to grow older without the person I was supposed to grow old with. Though I am not surprised, the last thing Colby was looking at on his phone was birthday gift ideas.

I never imagined that April 26th, my birthday, could be so painful. This was supposed to be my first birthday as a wife. 27 was going to be my year. I was married to my dream guy. We were about to buy a home. We were planning to start a family. We were supposed to have many more dinner dates, trips around the world, and so much time together. Colby was supposed to be here for all my birthdays until I turned at least 100! Colby loved my birthday much more than I loved my birthday. He always made it a big deal. He loved making me feel so special. All I wanted for my birthday was my husband back. I wanted him here. I knew he was probably celebrating up in Heaven, but I was completely broken down here on earth. Everyone was doing everything in their power to try and step up and make me feel special for him. Colby's billet family, and my two best friends, Alex and Kellie, made a video of them all singing to me. My hockey sisters sent me beautiful gifts. Family friends dropped off food. Although I appreciated everyone's gestures, at the time, I just didn't want any of it. Nothing was going to make anything about this birthday "happy." I will always be so grateful for the many milestones and celebrations I had with Colby; I just wish we could have had many more.

The physical part of grief is something I feel needs to be addressed, as it is far too often overlooked. Grief varies in many ways. For me, I was losing weight at a drastic pace. I have always been a small-framed person but within a few weeks after Colby's death I dropped to 87 pounds (39.4 kgs). It got to the point my doctor would have me "weigh in" until I got back over 100 pounds.

I also began to experience more physical symptoms. My body just seemed to be crashing. One night not long after my birthday, my breathing started to get worse. My heart felt like it was racing out of control and coming out of my chest. I was convinced I was dying and that was okay by me. My parents made the decision that I had to go to the hospital. The same hospital my husband was in and helicoptered out of. I did all I could to convince them not to take me. I hated hospitals. I still do. However, my parents weren't taking no for an answer. It was there I learned about another physical part of grief for the first time, "Broken Heart Syndrome". A heart condition often brought on by stressful situations and extreme emotions. It turns out this is common for widows to experience. Something I was now experiencing. Ironically, one of the emergency doctors that night was there the morning Colby got admitted. He talked to me about the dreadful morning. He shared how he was heartbroken for me. I will always appreciate that he took the time to enter into my pain. I told him it felt like I was dying too. He explained Broken Heart Syndrome is a real thing. They eventually were able to settle my heart rate down and discharged me. But honestly, my heart wasn't even close to being okay.

Looking back over those days after leaving the hospital, I can only describe myself as a walking zombie. Though there were a few things that seemed to be helping, such as medication for my anxiety, my therapist, and my family, I was learning more and more you can't heal grief. Turns out even Chester needed to be on anxiety medication. He kept searching for Colby and couldn't understand where he'd gone. It felt like a nightmare I couldn't wake up from. The rest of the world was functioning the best it could with the uncertainty of Covid, but I wasn't able to function at all. I wasn't able to shower or brush my teeth for days at a time. I refused to go outside or walk Chester. My Dad and Mom continued to show up for me in so many ways.

Covid made my grief so isolating and lonely. Normally, there would have been a funeral in the first few weeks, but at that point, we had no idea when we would even have one. I still couldn't hug any of our friends. I remember staring at my phone hoping I'd wake up from this nightmare to a text or call from Colby. That text never came. I would generically respond to everyone checking in on me that I was just going "second by second" but was trying my best to be brave for Colb. Because, if not with him then for him.

It took a few weeks for Colb's urn to arrive at the funeral home. His ashes had been sitting in cardboard boxes beside my bed. We took the boxes to the funeral home to transfer his ashes into the urn. I remember hugging the boxes so tightly. I didn't want to let them go but I eventually handed them over. I had also asked for three other smaller containers to be filled with his ashes for his family so they could decide what they wanted to do with them. I remember carrying his urn outside to the car. I kissed it. I hugged it. I just wanted to feel a real hug- one of his famous hugs one more time.

Not long after bringing his urn home, I finally got to hug one of his teammates. My first hug in weeks that wasn't from an immediate family member. Colby's teammate from the Oilers, Connor McDavid, and his girlfriend Lauren came to visit me. I will never forget them walking through the front door nor forget the power of those first hugs and tears. My grief was so delayed because of Covid. My parents made us dinner that night. It was just the 5 of us. I realized I was the 5th wheel. We talked about all that had happened. We talked about Colby and the man that he was. We cried a ton and even laughed a little. I always say that I feel Colby the most around his teammates. Hockey was our life. Our hockey family were our people. And now finally, being able to hug a couple of our people helped my heart more than I could ever rightly explain.

A few days prior to Connor and Lauren coming for dinner, I had decided to move back to Edmonton by the end of May. The Oilers were starting the memorial fund and I wanted to be there for that. I would have gone back to Boston, but the borders were still closed. I just knew I couldn't stay at my parents' house anymore. It had become too triggering. Dinner that night reminded me how important it was for me to be around people who understood the hockey life and could support me. I knew that Edmonton would welcome me back with open arms. We started looking for apartments online. I had to start from scratch. Colb and I had no furniture. I had half of our wedding gifts (that we had yet to open) at my parents. So here I was, a new widow, having to build a new life and new home all alone. Picking out house stuff was excruciating. I remember picking pink things. I hate the color pink. I would have never picked that. But I wanted everything "girly" and the opposite of what I would have picked had Colby still been alive.

I spent the next few weeks carefully packing all Colby's belongings and packing mine to be sent to Edmonton. One night as I was packing, I received an insightful message. It was from Colby's flight medic from the helicopter. He said something that I'll always hold close to my heart. He apologized for not letting me on the helicopter and explained how it was out of his control.

"This call will be forever in my memory in so many ways. Over 40 years in this profession and this one will always stand out. Your recuperation from this loss will be your life's greatest challenge."

This flight medic was right. The recuperation from losing Colby will always be my life's greatest challenge. Because death ends a life, but it doesn't end a relationship. A love and a marriage like ours doesn't just die. Despite Colby not physically being with me, I will always be his wife. Out of the billions of people on this planet, he chose me to spend the rest of his life with. The feeling of longing for Colb and realizing that I can't see him again on this earth will always be overwhelming and isolating. I realize the depth of my grief cannot be understood by anyone but myself. The intimacy in my grief kills me at times. The personal side is the deepest and most complicated. There's no sugar-coating grief. Deep down, I know all the sadness and unbearable pain grief brings is a result of our deep love for each other.

However, at the same time, I can't let it knock me down. I can't just allow it to keep me in bed day after day. That's not what Colb would have wanted for me. The way I hurt makes me realize how much I love Colby. It's a testament to our love and vows. I see life in a different light now than I did before. I see life in a way I would never have if Colb had never been a part of it. I cannot imagine my life without Colb, and I never want to. I want to have the courage to wake up every morning and watch how he continues to still be a part of my life from Heaven. How he continues to love me, challenge me, motivate me, strengthen me, and lead my life. One full of heartbreak, love, adventure, success, doubt, and unbelievable sadness. But also, one full of purpose to make something worthwhile while honoring the love of my life. I was born to love Colb. I know that and believe it with all my heart. Countless times he would say we had Agape love and that our story was the greatest love story this world has ever seen. The day he left this earth, I promised him in Heaven, I would continue to do my best and I know he is doing the same up there.

CHAPTER 12

Agape Love

"Agape. The highest form of love. Selfless. Sacrificial. Unconditional. Persists no matter the circumstance."

Colb and I always thought the words "I love you" never fully described the amount of love that we had for each other. Our love was hard to put into words. It was and continues to be a truly incredible and special kind of love. We loved each other so much more than just "I love you" so we decided to say Agape. What an honor it is to have such a love with Colb and share it with others.

I once heard,

"The word that is the secret to marriage and indeed all relationships is Agape. Agape is a special kind of love. Agape will get you through the ups and downs in a marriage. Agape listens. Agape heals. Agape gets up in the middle of the night when you're sick. Agape goes on adventures together. Agape supports the others' dreams. I pray that you'll be so good to each other, that you can remind us all that this is real. Love is real. And we're watching, we're cheering you on, and it starts with a secret, and the secret is Agape." - Unknown

It is a love that I hope everyone can find in their lifetime.

Love is displayed in many ways. It can be as simple as taking care of our loved one's belongings. My therapist recommended I pack up Colby's personal belongings and wait at least a year to decide what I wanted to do with them. It would provide me time until I was in a clearer frame of mind to decide things. I agreed and immediately started to roll up all Colb's clothes in suitcases for the very last time. I did not want anyone to help, I was protective of his things. I remember smelling every shirt, every pair of pants, every game-day suit, and every pair of socks before I carefully rolled them up in an organized manner into suitcases.

Colb had given me the title of being a professional packer, something most hockey wives become. He would always joke, once I was in the packing mood, no one could slow me down. I can't tell you how many times I had packed and unpacked in our relationship. Starting from a long-distance relationship, to moving in together, to every new season, to the trips we took, to the call-ups and downs from the NHL to the AHL. After every road trip when he came home, I'd unpack and repack his stuff, so it was ready to go in case it was "lucky" (aka he got a goal). Needless to say, I packed a lot. But this time was drastically different, it was the hardest pack of my life. It made me think of all the times I took for granted being able to roll up his clothes and pack them for him. Doing laundry for a loved one or packing for them may seem like just another chore but it is far more than that.

Days leading up to moving to Edmonton, I had a call from one of Colby's teammates, Cooper Marody. Cooper shared a life-changing memory he had with Colb. He explained that the two of them were the first to arrive in the locker room before a game. Colby knew Cooper was also a Christian so he decided to play Christian music instead of the normal, super loud pump-up music the guys would play. Although jamming out to Christian music in the locker was not the norm, Colb did it anyway. As Cooper shared, it truly was a testimony to how confident Colb was in his newfound faith, and he had no shame in sharing it. I can only imagine the two of them singing and dancing to Christian music together. As I continued to listen to Cooper share this story, it brought tears to my eyes. Colby didn't grow up going to church, yet here he was a fairly new Christian confident and comfortable enough in his faith to do this. It makes me so proud. It was also during this call when the idea of Cooper writing a song about Colby and myself came about. Cooper is an incredible singer. So, he decided right then and there that he would write a song and send it to me when he was done.

I remember the night before flying out to Edmonton. Cooper had finished the song. He said that it was one of the easiest songs he ever wrote. He told me he felt like Colb was giving him the words to write. I hid in my bedroom and listened to it all alone. It was perfect. I bawled. And then I bawled some more when I heard these lyrics:

"You wanna see me and I wanna see you but you still have some lovin' left to do. So, live it out and make me proud. Be everything and all you are. I'll take your hand in mine, I'll squeeze it three more times. But Em, until that day, Agape."

After hearing the song, I ran upstairs and played it for my parents, and shared it with a few of our close family friends. We all bawled, smiled, and bawled again. We felt Colby's presence in the room, and we heard Colb's own voice expressing his love to me in his vows. The words we heard, we knew Colby would truly say and want me to hear.

The song "Agape" had such an incredible impact, not just on me, but on so many lives. Our faith and love story began to enter homes across the world. People started reaching out saying how it touched their lives and has given them hope. It is incredible that in Colby's short life as a Christian, he has and continues to inspire others and give them hope. I know he must be in awe in Heaven.

Neither of us could have imagined our faith and love story would make such a difference and touch so many lives. The song was truly one of the best-treasured gifts I could have ever received. I might be a bit biased, but it is beautiful. If you haven't heard the song, I encourage you to do so.

Many people continue to still message me sharing pictures from all over the world where they see or hear the word, Agape. It is special. It is a beautiful reminder. I always appreciate seeing and hearing these stories. When I receive these messages, I feel like it is another way Colby is saying I love you from Heaven. I will never forget this past summer when the word Agape was the answer to the New York Times "Wordle of the Day." I woke up to so many messages from people saying they knew the word because of Colb, myself, and our story. Again, the power of Agape.

It had been about 7 weeks since Colb passed and the time had been filled with media interviews, news articles, and lots of isolation. It was such a lonely time. I remember one day, I walked up the stairs, I looked at my Mom, and all of the flowers around the house and I just said, "Get rid of them all". I didn't want to see or smell them anymore. I felt like I was suffocating. I just wanted to escape it all. I think I had convinced myself that being in Edmonton would be easier. I wouldn't be in the house that Colby got sick in. I would be surrounded by more of our people when the Covid restrictions were lifted. I had this hope for Edmonton that maybe my grief wouldn't be as bad there. Boy was I wrong. It was actually going to be harder. Way harder.

For weeks after Colb passed away, I'd wake up multiple times a night expecting him to be right next to me. It is funny how your mind works in times of grief in order to survive. I had convinced myself he was just on a long road trip. Just maybe he was going to be in Edmonton when I landed. But I'd realize very soon that I wasn't dreaming. This was all a nightmare. Colby wasn't on a road trip. He was gone and he wasn't coming back.

My last few days in Barrie before flying to Edmonton are difficult to put into words. I was ready to leave and to be honest, part of me never wanted to come back. The pain and the memories were just too much. However, when we were trying to book our flights to Edmonton, we found out there were strict rules when it came to flying ashes. It turns out we had to take Colby's ashes back to the funeral home where they would put them back into the boxes, and I would pack his urn in my checked luggage.

The morning had finally come to leave Barrie and move to Edmonton, although we were still in the middle of a global pandemic. It felt surreal. It had been 7 weeks since Colby died and somehow, I was still standing. I was hoping when I got to Edmonton things would start getting better and certainly felt things could not get worse.

I remember driving to the airport that morning clinching Colb's ashes. I was hugging them so tightly. Chester was attached to my hip, and he had no idea where we were going or what was happening. I remember going through security and having to show them Colb's death certificate. I had to open up the boxes with his ashes. It all felt so violating. I understand it's protocol, but it was just so hard. This was my husband. This was his body. I was made to feel like I was doing something wrong. I remember sitting on the plane with Colby's ashes at my feet and Chester in my arms. He was wrapped in the same blanket that I had the nurses give Colby during those four days in the hospital. I have a picture of that day. I look so tiny. I look so broken. I don't even recognize myself. I cried off and on during the flight. I felt like a shell of myself. I don't know how I was doing all the things I was doing. Especially with so many people watching my every move.

When my parents and I landed in Edmonton, the team driver picked us up from the airport. It was the same driver Colby and I often used, driving us back and forth to the airport during every call-up and down. I was so happy when I saw him, and he hugged me. During this time, you never knew who you could hug and who you couldn't. Hugs were all I really wanted. I can't even explain what that hug meant. Over the last 7 weeks, he was one of a handful of people that I got to hug. He shared a story during the drive about the first time he drove Colby to pick me up from the airport. He shared even though Colby had just seen me a few days before, how excited and giddy he was for me to join him in Edmonton. Reminiscing on what the driver shared, reminded me of how much Colb loved me, in a strange way it brought me a sense of happiness and warmth knowing he never hesitated to openly share how much he loved me. It is so important to remember our loved ones, to hear their name in conversations, and to be reminded how much they meant to others. Please, never stop sharing your memories or stop saying their names.

Looking back, if Colb and I were apart for even 15 minutes, we'd miss each other. A trip to the grocery store or a quick errand would often be met with a picture to each other with Chester saying, "I miss you." When Colb was on the road we talked every minute that he was free. We ended each call or text with "I miss you." I thought missing Colb was hard then but the way I miss him now is so much harder. It's a feeling of longing and emptiness all in one, I can't put into words. This missing him is so different but the loving Colb has stayed the same.

There is a saying "absence makes the heart grow fonder." I can only imagine how much my love for Colb will continue to grow and brighten as time goes on. This love, our love, was and is worth the pain. And even though my world was crumbled, and my heart was ripped open, it was all worth it. I believe that with all my heart. However, it was going to take everything I had within me to hold onto the glimpse of hope on the other side of this tragedy, my life could be beautiful again.

When my parents and I arrived at the hotel where Colby and I lived periodically over two hockey seasons, so many memories

Exploring our creative side during one of our many Christmases together.

Having fun in Newport, Rhode Island

Colb's first NHL game in Boston.
December 21, 2017

Winter Classic 2019 with my parents.
Bruins vs. Blackhawks

My 26th Birthday in Boston.
My last one with Colb.

Christmas 2019. Our first and last Christmas as a married couple.
(l-r) Chester, Colb, myself, my Dad, my sister Ky, Sydnie, my Mom, and
my brother-in-law Dave.

Colb's vows in his handwriting.
I'll cherish this forever!

The best day of our lives.
July 19, 2019

Honeymooning in Mexico.

The day we bought Chester.
Or as Colb liked to call him, Chestman!

Our last Halloween team party together.
Bakersfield, California

Colb's billet family visiting in Edmonton.
(l-r) Colb, Shayne, Brian, Dior, Kim, and myself.
Missing his billet brother, Jace.

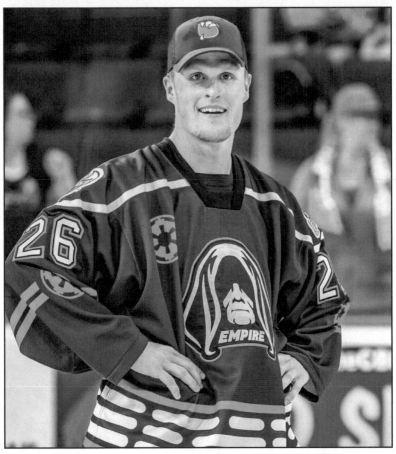

Colb's last hockey game (and his last goal). March 7, 2020. He would be in emergency brain surgery exactly a month later.

The scrimmage game in honor of Colb where all players wore his #12. This game made NHL history and is in the Hockey Hall of Fame.

The banners hung to create the walls of the
"NHL Bubble" in Edmonton.

Colb's Celebration of Life on April 10, 2021
at Rogers Place in Edmonton.

Colin and me in Philadelphia.

The Boit family. (l-r) Mary, Cutter, Peter, Jenny, James, Alex, McKenna, Chandler, myself, and Colin.

My family Christmas 2022 . (l-r) Colin, Sydnie, myself, Chester, my Mom, Olivia, my Dad, my sister Ky, and my brother-in-law Dave.

The real MVP of this book, Chester.

and waves of emotions flashed through my mind. The ladies who worked at the front desk had placed flowers in our room with a card. They welcomed Chester and me back with open arms and tears of sadness. After dropping off our suitcases and settling in a bit, I now had to deal with something else that I categorized as "one of hardest things". We headed over to the Edmonton Oilers' rink (Rogers Place) to get Colby's car. It had been parked in the player's parking area. It was filled with the winter clothes that we left in the car whenever we flew back and forth to play in California. I remember walking into the rink. I remember seeing for the first time TD Forss, the head athletic trainer, he had been watching over Colby's car. I watched him grab Colb's keys. As we were standing in the locker room, I could only imagine how hard it was for him. I cried so hard. Nothing made sense.

TD and his wife Monica had a special place in both Colby's and my heart. They were the first Oilers' couple that we really got to know and spend time with. Ironically, we ended up at the same resort as them during the All-Star break where we vacationed in Mexico. We spent several days with them by the poolside. That trip was one of our last trips together. It was where I took one of my favorite videos of Colby. Colb was always the life of the party and made the best out of every situation. One night, we ended up at the karaoke bar at the resort. By the end of the night, everyone was calling him the "karaoke man". They would be chanting my name to kiss him and to get up and dance with him on the dance floor. No denying that Colb was the adventurous, and extrovert one between the two of us. He taught me so much; he always encouraged me to "get out of my comfort zone". He always made me feel comfortable in uncomfortable situations by making me laugh or sometimes just forcing me to do it. After he died, I received messages from people we had met that week saying it was the funniest night of their vacation. That was Colb, always making others laugh. He brought me and so many others so much happiness. He lived life to the fullest and never took any moment for granted. I will always miss his spontaneous funny side.

Looking back, it is ironic that TD was one of the first people Colb and I got to know from the Oilers, and now he was the first person to meet me walking back into the rink as a broken widow. TD took us to the car; I will never forget the smell when we opened the door. It smelled just like Colb. The waves of emotions hit me like a tidal wave. It took all my strength to keep standing. How could this all be happening? The gut-wrenching realization I would never see my husband play in this rink again, I would never park in the player's parking lot or walk to the car with him after a game was unbearable.

As we headed back to the hotel, Colby's absence became even more profound. It was the first time driving in his car without him, the lingering smell, the same route we had taken so many times from the rink to the hotel after games were too hard to grasp. I tried to convince myself that he was just on a really long road trip, or maybe he was just waiting for me somewhere else in Edmonton, but he wasn't.

I often was told how strong I was and how brave I was not to give up. The truth is my strength came from knowing and experiencing Agape love - love, and faith that persists regardless of the circumstances. I hated the fact that death had separated us, but I knew with all my heart our love will always remain. Our faith assured me that as each day passed, it also meant I would be one day closer to being with him again. Agape.

CHAPTER 13

Edmonton

There are no words to describe how I felt waking up that first morning in Edmonton. It didn't seem real I was moving into a new place without Colb. This was the first time in my life that I'd be living alone. And this was all happening during a global pandemic. One of the things I flew to Edmonton for my new apartment was one of Colby's hot sauce bottles. It wasn't going to expire for another two years and Colb LOVED hot sauce. I did not have the heart to throw away the hot sauce bottle or the chili flakes that he used to make avocado toast for me each morning. Eventually, they both expired so I would throw them out. I would sob my eyes out because it felt like I was throwing Colby away too. I had made a rule with Colb that if he bought one thing, we would donate one thing. He loved to shop but I hated having clutter. And here I was, not able to throw out a single thing.

The survivors' guilt and the fear of him being forgotten were really hard emotions for me, and they still are. These emotions influenced many of my decisions, big or small, right down to keeping his hot sauce bottle. There were times I would picture Colb in Heaven, trying to comfort me with that big famous smile of his saying, "Thank you for continuing my life story, our love story. Please continue to make me proud and go be happy… and throw out my old hot sauce bottle ya goof." But I wasn't quite ready. I just placed it in my fridge and waited two more years before I could even think about doing that.

During the first few days back in Edmonton I tried to get "settled" and make this new place feel like a home. What I quickly began to realize was the profound truth in the saying, "home is not a place but a person." Nothing was going to feel like home without Colb. I was never going to be the same. I felt like I was never going to feel at home again. My life now had a before and an after. Before Colb's death and after Colb's death. Only a handful of our friends were in Edmonton, and many couldn't come to visit because of the restrictions. However, after getting settled in a bit, and some restrictions had been lifted, I had my first visitors, Colby's billet parents, Kim and Brian. It had been almost two months since Colb had died. They decided to make the long 7-hour drive from Swift Current. They were like family and wanted to support me and said they couldn't stay away any longer. It meant so much to me. It was not the first time his billet parents made that long drive or took a flight to Boston to support Colb and me. One memory of their unconditional love and support happened in February 2019. I called Kim and shared that Colb and I were dealing with a particular situation that had become very hurtful to the both of us, and that Colb was taking it really hard. Both Kim and Brain dropped everything and drove 7 hours throughout the night, in a snowstorm, to come and talk with us. It ended up they could only visit Colb for about 30 minutes as he had to prepare for a game that night. However, I know those 30 minutes meant the world to Colb, something he never forgot for the rest of his short-lived life here on this earth. They were and will always be much more than billet parents, they were part of our family.

I will never forget our first hugs, the many uncontrollable tears, and the late-night talks of so many sweet memories of Colb. The weekend went by so fast, and I hated to say goodbye. However, true to who they were, they made the trip again, two weeks later. This time, they brought Colby's two little billet sisters, Shayne and Dior. Our two flower girls at our wedding less than a year ago. Like I said at the beginning of the book, Kim and Brian were an incredible influence that helped mold Colby into the man he became at such a young age.

It was not long after their visit that I received triggering news about Chester. Chester had been having knee problems for a while. Actually, the day before Colb was taken away in the ambulance, we were trying to get on a zoom call with a local vet to figure out what was happening. Chester was doing this thing where he would yelp in pain and his back knees would lock. He would try and shake them out, but you could tell something was wrong. After taking him to the vet in Edmonton we were told that he needed double knee surgery. He wasn't even a year old. It was going to be a long recovery. It was going to be painful for Chester, but we had no other option. So here I was, booking surgery for Chester in the midst of everything else that was happening around me.

I remember leading up to that day feeling so guilty that he had no idea what was coming. He was already struggling with separation anxiety, so I didn't want to leave his side. I was petrified of any surgery, knowing Colby never woke up from his. Chester was the last meaningful thing that I had left of Colby. The night before the surgery, I put Chester's blanket (that Colby had in the hospital), over Colby's pillow which still had not been washed. Chester slept on top of it all night. This is how he sleeps every night now. The night before his knee surgery, I remember having this overwhelming feeling, IF Chester died in surgery, that meant that I could die too. I didn't have anything left of Colby's here to live for. We could all be reunited in Heaven. I don't mean this in a way of animal cruelty at all. I just always felt that as long as Chester was living, I couldn't leave him. I didn't want him to lose both his parents. He was the only thing that would keep me living.

Chester did make it out of surgery. He came home with two bright-colored casts on both his back legs. He wouldn't be able to walk for a while. We would have to hold him up to go to the bathroom. It would take weeks for him to recover. Every time I would hear him throw up, I would freeze, and it reminded me of Colby puking his final night. You could tell Chester was in so much pain. I felt helpless. Colby wasn't here and I felt like a shell of myself, trying to keep it all together.

People continued to tell me how strong I was and how our love story was changing lives. Here was the thing, although I appreciated all the support and thoughtfulness, I didn't want all the messages, calls, and support. I didn't want my Instagram to grow. I didn't want any of it. I didn't want to have to be "strong" or "inspire" others. All I ever wanted was to live a full life with Colb and die old together. But here I was, a widow, with all our future plans and everything I knew shattered. To be honest, knowing I couldn't turn back time, I wanted more than anything to speed it up so I could go meet Colb in Heaven. Life just didn't seem worth living. I could barely see any of our friends. Our dog was incredibly ill. The media was all over me. There was a global pandemic. I just wanted the nightmare to end.

During this time, an announcement I had dreaded was about to happen. The NHL would be resuming. This crushed me. Yes, I knew that hockey needed to go on. Yes, I knew that many of the players and their families were super excited to get back out there. Yes, I knew this was good for the hockey community as a whole. But no, I wasn't looking forward to any of the things that would come with this announcement. It was just another reminder I'd never see Colb again. The thought of never seeing Colb on the ice again was beyond hurtful. The realization I wouldn't be able to celebrate any more of his career milestones was so hard to handle. To be honest, selfishly, I didn't want hockey to start again. And I wondered if Colby dying, it meant that hockey "died" along with him. I wondered if our hockey family was still going to be family or not. I wasn't the player. I was just the wife.

I'd quickly learn that wasn't the case. Not even close. Every single team, player, coach, staff, and family member rallied around me. They say, "honor a man by the way you treat his widow." And that's exactly what our hockey family did and continues to do. I felt so guilty for being jealous and not happy about the season restarting. It was a constant battle. And to be honest, at times, it still is. Seeing all our friends still playing, but not being on a "team" has been one of the biggest adjustments for me. So instead of being at the games, on the road, prepping for the next move, I was at home spending most nights alone crying on the couch. I wasn't ever going to hear "Colbbbyyy Caveee" from announcers again. I was never going to see a little redheaded baby wearing a "Daddy" jersey with Colb's number. The NHL restarting made so many people happy but for me, it was excruciating.

With the NHL restarting, and the fact that Covid was on the increase and wasn't going away, the "NHL bubble" went into effect. Edmonton and Toronto were two of the cities that were picked to be "host" cities while the bubble was in play. That meant that not only was the NHL restarting but it was going to be starting again in the city I just moved back to. I was going to be in the same building as some of our best friends I hadn't been able to see since Colby died.

I had no idea how much the NHL season restarting would affect my grief. In a beautiful gesture, the NHL and the Oilers would start the hashtag #WeSkateForColby during the playoffs. Banners saying "We Skate for Colby" were placed all around downtown Edmonton. Everywhere I looked I'd see Colby's name. My deceased husband's name. It was beautiful but heartbreaking all at the same time. For three months, as the NHL continued its season in the bubble, the large banners with his name would be on display. I was SO honored that the NHL and hockey community rallied around Colby the way that they did. It just showed again how incredible my husband was, not just as a hockey player, but as a person. It makes me more proud than any Stanley Cup ring Colb could have ever won. At the same time, it was really hard to walk out of my apartment's front door. My deceased husband's name was everywhere I went. However, over some time it did become a comfort thing for me. I began to walk out of my building and say, "Morning Colb." Often you could find Chester and myself sitting by one of the banners with his name on it. As I said, it became a comfort thing like a security blanket for me. It was nice to know that he hadn't been forgotten.

The NHL used the hashtag #WeSkateForColby, but personally, I began to use #WeLiveForColby because he was so much more than just a hockey player.

CHAPTER 14

Our One-Year Wedding Anniversary

I remember our wedding week like it was yesterday. The excitement of our dream finally coming true. Colby seeing me in my dress. Celebrating with all of our loved ones. Now here I was, a year later, three months since Colb died, not knowing when I would even be able to have a funeral for my husband. I didn't want our anniversary to come. I didn't want to celebrate it. How do you celebrate the love of your life when the love of your life isn't here to celebrate it with? Leading up to the 19th, I went through countless pictures, letters, and videos. Looking back, I feel like I never wrote enough, said enough, or took enough pictures. I just wanted my husband back. I walked down the aisle to "I Get to Love You" by Ruelle. Our first dance was to "Making Memories of Us" by Keith Urban. The week leading up to our wedding I listened to these songs on repeat. And the week leading up to our anniversary, I did the same. And the lyrics that stood out most were these:

"I promise that I'll never leave. When it's too heavy to carry, remember this moment with me."

"I'm gonna be here for you from now on this you know somehow. You've been stretched to the limits but it's alright now. And I'm gonna make you a promise, if there's life after this, I'm gonna be there to meet you with a warm, wet kiss."

I longed for one more kiss. For one more dance. As I said, the few days leading up to our wedding anniversary were painful. There were so many people in my life trying to fill a void that was unfillable. At times I appreciated it. At times I would get annoyed that no one seemed to understand. I remember on the 18th, the day before our anniversary, my parents and I were coming back from running an errand, and sitting outside of my building were Loni and Matt with flowers. Matt had grown up with Colby. Although they were from Calgary, they wanted to let me know they were thinking about me. They went above and beyond. They made the long drive (over three hours) just to drop off flowers. They would actually end up staying over and we shared the bottle of champagne that the two of them had given us on our wedding day. It was fitting that they were there to celebrate with me. These two have continued to go above and beyond and I will forever be grateful that Colby brought them into my life.

I always had this image of Colby being confused when he got to Heaven. But after God explained to him why he was there and why his life needed to be cut short, he'd understand. And then he'd shift his entire focus to watching over me and making sure I was okay. That would be his biggest worry. I just know if any of my friends or family beat me to Heaven, the first question Colby is going to ask them is if Em and Chester are okay?

For the longest time, I nagged and asked Colby and my Dad what they talked about when Colby asked him to marry me in Nashville. Neither of them would tell me. But right before our anniversary, my Dad said that one of the things Colby said that drew him to me was my faith. He loved that I went to church. He loved that I got him to go to church. He loved that I had a relationship with the Lord. It was different than what he had ever known. This broke my heart but filled it at the same time. As hard as it was knowing he was in Heaven without me, I knew that I had to keep being the woman he married. "Attracted to my faith" he would tell my Dad. My faith felt completely broken, but at the same time, my faith caused me to know I was going to see him again one day in Heaven. In Colby's vows, he said, "I can't wait to spend eternity with you." I am going to spend eternity with Colb. And I can't wait for that day to come because him choosing me to be his wife will always be my biggest honor and no one can take that away from me. He is the reason I still have breath in my lungs. He is the reason I get out of bed every day. He is the reason I will get up again and again. I will climb up out of rock bottom. I will rise. I will continue to strive to change so many children's lives with his memorial fund. I am changed because of him. He helped me feel worthy of love, and even though he's no longer here with me, his love is mine to keep.

The 19th came and I felt like everyone was watching me. Just waiting to see how I was going to react. We ordered pizzas from my rooftop. Dave Tippett and Jay Woodcroft, two of Colby's coaches, came and gave me hugs before they headed into the NHL bubble. Four of Colby's former teammates would too. All the young guys that he played with in Bakersfield. I sent three balloons (three hands squeezes) up to Heaven for him. I wrote on each balloon and released them while Agape was playing. Colby's youngest billet sister, Dior, was by my side the entire time because she wanted to make sure someone took care of me since Colby was gone. I just remember holding onto Chester and crying a ton. I read my vows over and over again. Those vows won't ever change. From then, to tomorrow, to 10 years from now, until the day we meet again.

Because I can't wait to spend eternity with Colb, and each day here is one day closer to seeing him in Heaven.

These were the vows I wrote to Colb on our wedding day. Vows that still remind me how blessed I was to have him as my husband.

"Colby, you came into my life at the most perfect time. A few days after meeting you, I remember telling my Mom and sister that I had found my person and that I was going to marry you. My greatest hope in life after that was that you would feel the same way. You would be the kind of person that would make me laugh in the hard times, that would be full of integrity, and be a hard worker, and support me in all my dreams, as well as my Prosecco, tea lattes, and avocado toast addiction. But the truth is, you've been so much more than that. You are hardworking, wise, humble, and everything else I could ever want in a husband. It will be an honor to be your wife on the good days, and there is no one else I want to battle through the tough days with. So, before God and standing here in front of our family and friends, I promise to walk with you through the highs, and hold you through the lows as long as we both live. I promise to create a loving, and encouraging home for our future children because they are a chapter of our love story that I am so excited for. I promise to be faithful. I promise to pursue you every day of our lives while being patient and selfless. I promise to challenge you to be the best person you can be while supporting the gifts that God gave you. I promise to be your best friend and greatest love. I promise to buckle up on this crazy journey to wherever hockey life takes us. Because whatever city, or country we are in, I know with you I am home. I promise to cherish and love you unconditionally because you have my full heart and I dedicate my whole life to showing you as well. I am so excited to officially be your wife within the next few minutes. I have prayed for you and this moment for as long as I can remember. I love you forever and always."

No words I can say in this chapter will ever be able to describe the pain I was feeling. This post is the closest thing to being able to express my love for Colb from afar. No flowers from family or friends could help. No one could make it better:

"A year ago was the happiest day of our lives. We had the most beautiful day surrounded by our loved ones. It was the best day of my life; other than the day I see you again. Today, was one of the worst, only beaten by one. April 11th, I took my last breath with you and haven't been able to exhale since. The pain has pushed past vital organs and has settled deep into my bones. I don't know how, but I'm somehow living with my heart ripped out of my body. You should be here with me to celebrate. I can't help but think about all the things and experiences we will never have. It makes me want to puke, scream, cry, and shake, every time I think about not seeing you as a Dad. I will never be the same. When I was little, I was taught to protect my heart. To only give my heart to someone who could protect, guard, and love it. That's what you did, you were the glue that held my heart together. That's why today hurts so much more. Half my heart is with you in Heaven, it will always be, and the other half is shattered here. Despite being in Heaven, I believe you're still holding my broken heart, treasuring it, and taking care of it, better than I ever could for myself, especially now. Even though we're not physically together, you continue to be an incredible husband, Colb. I just wish you were here so bad; I would do anything. I'm so lucky to be your wife and I will continue to live out our vows to one another until we are reunited. So, here's to you, on our 1st year anniversary, my husband, my best friend, my other half, and my absolute hero. I miss you more than words can describe. Today is beyond unbearable. I'm not even close to being okay. But I do know one thing, my love for you and honoring your legacy is keeping me afloat. I will always be yours, Colb. You were the best thing to ever happen to me. You were so excited to make me a Cave. It will always be my biggest honor to be Mrs. Colby Alexander Cave. Agape, my love. One day closer to seeing you in Heaven."

I eventually went to bed that night. I made it through another "milestone" in my grief. However, the grief was even heavier. I was starting to learn that after every event there was a "grief hangover." You were even more mentally, physically, and emotionally, exhausted than you were on the actual day and event. The anticipation was over. The hovering of all the family, friends, media, and others was slightly calmer even though still there.

And then came the crash. Or at least that's what I thought would happen. But that wouldn't last long as I'd have to regroup because just as I would be getting through one milestone, there would be another one just around the corner. Each time I thought I could catch my breath, something would come to drown me again. Over and over and over. There was always a "next thing" that would take me down. It was never-ending. And I was just so tired.

CHAPTER 15

I Didn't Plan to Still Be Here

At the beginning of 2020, I ordered a new weekly planner. I was so excited because it was the first planner that had "Emily Cave" inscribed on it. After Colb died I couldn't even look in it because it was filled with OUR plans for 2020. All the important dates, vacations we'd booked, and every single thing that we'd planned for the year was written in it. What we hadn't planned on was for Colb to die tragically and suddenly. What we hadn't planned for was this global pandemic canceling everyone's plans. Needless to say, I ordered a new planner after he died. I just couldn't even stomach looking at all the ruined plans that 2020 had already brought into my life.

It was the middle of July, a few months after Colb had died and I found myself staring at a blank planner. I had nothing to fill it with. I had nothing to look forward to. I'd anticipated a calendar full of amazing adventures with Colb and instead, I was filling it with doctor appointments for weigh-ins, therapy sessions, appointments for Chester, and online appearances that I was to do for the media in Colby's honor. I remember thinking to myself, if I can just make it through these things in Colby's honor, if I can just make it to September, the season will be over, we can finally have Colby's funeral, and then I could go meet him in Heaven. I thought I would have been done with all my death duties as his wife, the funeral would be behind us, and his memorial fund would be up and running. I didn't plan to be here in September 2020. I didn't want to be here. I didn't see any reason for me to be here.

Little did I know at the time, this new weekly planner may have saved my life. It seems weird to say, but it is true. Somehow, this weekly planner began to fill up more and more as time passed. It became filled with coffee dates with new friends in my building. With more events that honored Colb. With amazing friends that came to visit. Having something to look forward to keep me going. After more time passed, I started to grasp I was still here for a reason. It was through so many people's prayers, my faith, and I have to Colb cheering me on from Heaven, I am still here. And even though many days I didn't want to be here, I began to realize that there was a reason I still was.

A few days after our first wedding anniversary, the Oilers hosted a scrimmage game in Colby's honor. Every player wore #12. This was going to be the last time I ever saw my husband's number on the ice. Gut-wrenching and unfair do not begin to describe my emotions leading up to the game. I should have been watching Colby. He should have been out there wearing #12. But I was so humbled and honored to get to watch his brothers wearing his number. The NHL invited his family, my parents, and myself. His family declined the offer due to having prior plans. However, Colby's billet parents and two billet sisters were still in town visiting, so they came to support my parents and I instead. It was so nice to have them there. That morning, I laid out his jersey that the Oiler's wives gave me to wear for charity events during the previous seasons. I knew this would be the last time I would wear it. Colby's youngest billet sister held my hand walking into the scrimmage game. This wasn't a hockey milestone that I wanted to be a part of. A hockey milestone that was so big that it hadn't been done before in NHL history. This game would end up in the Hockey Hall of Fame. It may not be the Stanley Cup we dreamed about, but I was so proud of the NHL, the hockey community, and the rest of the world for honoring how incredible my husband was not just as a hockey player but as a person. I know I say that a lot throughout the book, but it is true. His legacy, the Memorial Fund, and the impact he made makes me more proud than any Stanley Cup ring. Right before the game began, his teammates skated over to the end of the ice and looked up at where we were standing and waved at us. Leon made a heart with his hands, and I lost it. I just wanted to hug them all so badly. They started the clock of the game at 12:12. It was a beautiful tribute to Colby. This would be the first of many tributes made to Colby over the next few months.

Before the playoffs started, the Oilers hung Colby's jersey outside their locker room. It's still hanging there today. Players touch it on the way out to the ice before they play. Here's the thing, his teammates, this city, the fans, and all the amazing people around the world were grieving Colb as well. They were forever changed by his story. By our story. These people were keeping me afloat. I knew Colby is so grateful looking down knowing they were taking care of me. I could feel the brokenness in some of the ones I did get to hug, but they were doing all that they could to be strong for Colb and me. I knew they were all playing for Colb. They were helping me make sure that Colby would never be forgotten because as his wife, that has always been my biggest fear. Colby being forgotten.

My parents left a few days after this game to go back to Barrie. They hadn't left my side in almost four months. They needed to get back to their house, my Dad was still trying to work full-time from Edmonton. I remember the day they left wondering how I was going to do this. Most of our friends were now in the NHL bubble. I just felt so alone. People seemed to worry about me and my "widow brain." I would forget so many things. Big and small. I'd forget to lock the doors. I'd accidentally leave the oven on. I forgot my phone number. I didn't know how I would handle being alone but somehow I convinced my parents that I needed to try. I knew they were worried, but I told them that I would be fine. Deep down, I knew I wasn't going to be. But I needed to try.

I remember the first few hours after they left, it took every cell in my body to shower and get dressed. At this point, none of my clothes fit me. I was so tiny. I had to buy kids' clothes if I wanted anything to fit. I didn't want to go outside or get fresh air, but I knew I had to. Chester had become my emotional support dog when Colby died. I would not go anywhere without him. I wouldn't even go to the lobby and get my mail without him. I was petrified of being alone. I decided to go to one of the drug stores close to me as I needed to fill my anxiety prescription and pick something else up. I will never forget being aggressively confronted by one of the security workers. She was asking for Chester's documentation. I was so nervous. I had hardly talked to anyone in the last few months let alone a stranger who was upset with me. As I was trying to fumble through my phone to pull up all of Chester's documentation the security officer verbally attacked me. She said that I didn't look like I needed an emotional support dog and that there was no point in me trying to pull up the paperwork because "You will just get away with it anyways because your husband's name is hung up all over the city." I froze. This young lady had no idea. Here I was dressed in children's clothes. It took everything in me to even step outside and walk into a store. Her hateful words shook me to the core, I just started crying. And then additional security officers showed up. I left the store immediately. I walked back to my apartment alone passing the banners around the city with my deceased husband's name written all over them.

I texted the Oilers team doctor and my therapist. I told them I was not okay. I texted my parents that as well. They had just landed back in Ontario. I told them I never wanted to leave my apartment again. And I didn't for a few days. I had a friend in my building come walk Chester for me. I just didn't want to leave. I knew people were watching me and some of those people were judging me. I had no privacy anymore. That first night all alone was so hard. My heart felt like it was going to explode. But somehow, I made it. I made it through my first day without him and without anyone else to help me. It was just Chester and me. We did it.

After a few days of being alone, I regained my confidence, and I went to go see some of Colby's former teammates that now played for other teams. Because of the restrictions, there was a barrier between us. I was thrilled to get to see familiar faces. I was able to give them hats that I had gotten made in honor of Colb to wear during the playoffs. There were so many of them to see. Milan Lucic, Adam Lowry, and Austin Czarnik, just to name a few. They were all special teammates of Colby's, and I will never forget seeing Ryan Donato for the first time. We were 6 feet apart and there was a tall barrier between us. The security worker took the hat and wiped it off before handing it to Ryan. I remember Ryan asking, almost begging the worker if he could come out of the "cage" and give me a hug. Obviously, that was not allowed. It was so inhumane. It was so unfair. Looking at all our people in the caged walls for the first time since Colb died and I still couldn't even give them a friggin' hug. Nothing about this was normal grieving.

Most mornings when I woke up before I'd walk Chester, I would mix Baileys in with my tea just to give me some courage. I would always wear a hat and sunglasses. But that disguise didn't seem to work very well. I was always stopped. 99% of the people were nice. Though it was done with such kindness it was still emotionally draining. I felt like I was always having to be "on", and I just didn't want to live like this anymore. On the days when I didn't think I could go one more hour, someone would drop something off or someone would show up unexpectedly. Caitlyn, one of my close friends, would come over just to wash my hair and bring me meals. Otherwise, I wouldn't eat. Joelle, another close friend of mine, would drop off flowers, tea lattes, and candy, and just come sit with me and Chester. It is so hard for grievers to tell their people what they need. It is too exhausting so people just showing up and checking in were the best things for me. I'm so grateful to those that just showed up. I wasn't going to ever ask them to. I wasn't going to tell them what I needed because most days, I had no idea. So, if you know someone who is grieving, show up for them. Don't ask for permission. Don't wait for an invitation because it'll never come. Just show up.

My therapist told me one day, "Em, your situation isn't just rare. It's monumental. There will never be a case like yours in the world". The rarity of Colb's death, the global pandemic, the public eye, the fact that it had been months and there had been no funeral, it was all just so rare. Though I had connected with a ton of other widows, my situation still seemed so different. And most times I still felt all alone. Then one day, one of my widowed sisters, Michelle, would text me something that changed my perspective:

"You can do hard things. You already know that. The struggle is the desire to continue and keep doing it. But we all need you here to continue sharing Colb with us all. So have your tough day and we'll all be waiting for you."

I remember thinking how right she was. If I didn't decide to continue to live, who would share about Colb? Who would carry his torch? I was left with this responsibility and at times it was so incredibly hard to carry. But I was the one that needed to do it. That night, the first game in the bubble, the Oilers and NHL held a moment of silence for Colby before they started the game. I didn't know this was going to happen. I wasn't even watching the game but my friend and the head coach's wife, Wendy Tippett texted me about it. I was walking Chester at the time, so I paused in the middle of the sidewalk and watched it all go down on my phone. Seeing this tribute to my husband was incredible. These tributes and stories helped me stay alive. The legacy Colb left behind continues to leave me speechless. He would be so humbled by it all. However, every time things like this would happen, every tribute to Colb, seemed to break my heart even more.

It was August when I was contacted about Colb's documentary. They planned to air it during the Stanley Cup finals. It felt like just when I got through one media thing, there was another one around the corner. When I heard that they wanted to do this, I broke down. My heart felt like it had been thrown into a blender and I was suffocating all at once. But at the same time, I was so incredibly humbled and honored that they wanted to do this. It took me a few days to process it all. There was already a memorial fund, a song, a scrimmage game in his honor, a Caver clothing line, a bracelet, and a moment of silence, and now they wanted to do a documentary, all within 5 months of his death. But we still hadn't had a funeral. I don't know why that bothered me so much. Maybe I felt that would add closure. Maybe I felt that would be my final duty when it came to the business side of death. I just know that it bothered me so much that so many things were being done to honor him but that we couldn't have a funeral.

The documentary consisted of three letters written and narrated by me. A letter to Colb. A letter to our hockey family. A letter to the future and the children that I wanted to help with his memorial fund. It was just last summer I was writing my wedding vows to him. Sometimes life just isn't fair. But here is the thing I kept reminding myself, our love story doesn't end just because Colb is in Heaven. He's still my husband. I'm still madly in love with him. We still have the greatest love story. We always will. It has inspired hundreds of thousands around the world. Although I was living a life here that we never planned, Colb was giving me more courage than I ever thought could fit into my five-foot-five-inch frame. He's still taking care of me in so many ways and I know he will continue until we are reunited. But my goodness, I just couldn't wait to run into his arms, grab his face, and kiss him again. But for now, I was here, and I needed to do all that I could to honor the man he was and the story of his life. Colb's life was incredibly special, and I'm forever lucky he chose me to be his wife. I was completely broken but was thrilled to be allowed to continue to share a glimpse of how amazing my husband was. I worked on these letters for weeks and in September a film crew would fly out to shoot the finished product.

Joelle and Caitlyn would spend that whole day with me so I wouldn't be alone. We filmed for 8 hours. I remember feeling like there was nothing left in me after we were done. I had given it my all. I just hoped that I had made Colby proud. I knew he would live on in the stories I told that day and continue to share on my Instagram. I didn't know the exact date I would be reunited with him, but I knew right then that there was a reason it wasn't September like I originally planned. There was a reason I was still here. And it was for my "why."

CHAPTER 16

Cyber Bullying

Oh, the things I could say in this chapter. There are so many things to say. But I'm going to do my best to be graceful while at the same time, sharing some truth. I know this book will bring more hate my way. I know many people will judge me and my grief journey even more. It'll be just like it's always been since the day Colby passed; I have been judged. Even when Colby was still in the hospital, I received hate mail. I've been told countless times that I am using his death for "fame." Let me tell you once again that, "you honor a man by the way you treat his widow." And by hiding behind a screen, starting rumors, and tearing a young widow apart, you're a coward. I know, I told you that I was going to try to be graceful here, but I had to get that out. This narrative some people spread that I'm using Colby's death for fame is sickening. Take a moment and think about that accusation. You're literally saying I knew he was going to die, and I was planning to become famous from losing my best friend and husband. It's not even logical. This was just one of the many horrible rumors were said about me.

However, every single time I heard something harsh being said, I would remind myself what Colby nicknamed me. His little world changer. I knew I needed to continue to be honest and vulnerable for all the other people, especially the widows, who may not have the voice or platform I had been given. Don't get me wrong, there has been much more positive media, and messages compared to negative media and messages. It's all the positive media, messages, comments, and articles that have truly kept me alive and moving forward today. Reading other people's journeys and how I have inspired them through our story has been truly remarkable. So, thank you to all of those that have shown me so much love over the last few years. I can't even begin to explain how much each and every message has meant to me. That being said, it wasn't all positive. And it was actually quite scary at times.

As I said, the media was involved from the moment Colby went into the hospital. This was not my doing. This was the NHLs. This just came with the territory of Colby being in the public eye and being a professional athlete. Again, I didn't ask for the media to provide updates. I didn't ask for the media to get involved. I was told that's how it was going to be. There was no other option for me. And because of that, I immediately lost my identity. I was labeled Colby Cave's widow. From the day he died, that's how people addressed me. I never knew that Colby's death would be in People Magazine or on the Today Show. My biggest issue with the media was that they just take whatever they want at times to make their narrative better. I never got any say. I remember one of Colby's teammates warning me and my parents about what to expect and how the media would be really hard on me.

Colby had experienced a bit of this. The media in Edmonton, certain reporters, and a handful of fans were really hard on him. It wasn't just him. It was and is all the players. They seem to forget that these players are human beings with feelings and with families. One of our best couple friends in Boston, Kaitlyn and Noel Acciari, shared with us that every mean tweet or comment they read, they would read it out loud. Colby and I had started that practice before he died. It helped us disengage from the actual words. I remember when Colby died, my Mom reached out to one of the reporters and called them out. It was a reporter who was really hard on Colb when he was alive but now that he was gone, he was praising him of course. Again, it fit his narrative and led to more clicks. He was using Colby's death for his benefit. And he wasn't the only one behaving in such a selfish manner.

I had assumed and down deep hoped that as time went on the hate would fade away. But I was so wrong in that assumption. As months went by it almost felt like it was getting worse. People became entitled and acted as if I owed them something. Overnight it was as if people became professionals in my life and my grief. The judgment was disgusting. Time and time again, it took a toll on me. I can't remember who it was, but someone shared this with me: "If a griever continues to talk about their deceased loved one, instead of asking "why haven't they moved on?", consider switching the question to "why is this bothering me?" Often, it's about our own discomfort with pain and struggle, not theirs. My close family and friends would remind me all the time that "hurt people hurt people" but this was personal. This was the most personal thing you could be hated and judged for - the death of your husband and best friend.

Here are only a handful of comments that have been sent to me over the last 2.5 years:

"Sorry, he is not going to make it out of this one. The next time you will see him, he will be in a body bag. Even if he makes it out, you will be wiping his butt and out cheating on him while he drools watching the Price is Right."

"Parlaying the loss of a loved one into an influencer lifestyle. The Edmonton Oilers and NHL are not helping. This is grief porn. Desperate. Sad. Gross Even."

"You just want pity. You might be the most attention-hungry person on earth... seek help."

"You are causing Colby extreme anguish up in Heaven. That HAS to make you feel bad!!"

"You didn't even know Colby. You only knew him for a few years. We knew him longer. You were only his wife for less than a year."

"You are extremely underweight. You are a slutty ugly ginger c*nt. I hope you never find happiness again. No man will ever want you."

"It should have been you."

"Do you truly even miss your husband? Stop pretending to be so sad and grieving. It is pathetic. You are pathetic."

"So, is the trick to get an ugly athlete to marry you and then pray he dies?"

"Mom of a dog. How silly! You will never have a real child with your dead husband. Get over it."

"Eat a sandwich, b*tch!"

"At what point do you stop feeling sorry for yourself?"

"Colby would be ashamed of you."

"F*CK you. F*CK your marriage."

This is just a handful of them. I have a whole folder on my computer. Some are even harsher than these believe it or not. It was incredibly hurtful to have some of these traced back to the senders and see who was behind some of these comments. Even though I knew all of these weren't true. Every word rocked me to my core. I didn't know if I was going to be able to recover from it. I didn't know if I even wanted to. Not only did I lose my husband, but now I'd lost my identity. If words could kill, I'd be gone. And to be honest, I wanted to die after hearing some of the things people said. I began to question everything. Were these people right? Did Colb even love me? Was I really a horrible wife? Should it have been me who died? Was Colby ashamed of me for who I'd become?

It's scary how someone can say something about something they know nothing about, but you still take it personally. Your brain can play tricks on you. Words hurt greatly. Actions or inactions of people hurt greatly. I am not saying I have never said anything hurtful. Heck, I'm far from perfect and I know that I've hurt others with my words. It's the aftermath and the way you handle a situation that speaks more volumes than maybe the hurtful words or actions said or done. Right now, all I know is that there is so much hurt and hate in the world. So many people are barely hanging on. I see it everywhere. People are really struggling. That's one of the reasons I tried so hard to continue to be open and honest about my journey on social media. I wanted people to know it's ok to hurt but also that you're loved and worthy. I tried so hard to reclaim the words used against me and to cut me down when I was already at rock bottom. I felt like I'd become a spokesperson for being "strong" for so many people, while at the same time feeling the complete opposite of strong. But somehow, someway my platform has brought a lot of strength to others and for that I am thankful. I realized I had been thrown into this new life and to be honest, at times I still feel like I am winging it. One thing has been made clearer to me over time, is I can never go back to my old life or the old me. That girl wasn't capable of seeing this trauma and loss before it rocked her world. That girl wouldn't have known how to protect or handle herself the way I have now learned.

In some strange way, helping others by being open about my journey was helping me. It was helping keep me alive even though some continued to feel the need to continue to judge me for it. You wouldn't judge someone for doing whatever they had to do to stay alive if they had a physical illness- like take insulin, chemo, have surgery, etc. Grief is mental and emotional, and people can't see the pain so there is a stigma around grief today's society and all I was doing was trying to break it down. I was trying to help others realize it is normal not to be ok. There is no blueprint or no timeline for grief and how it's supposed to look.

I remember one night right before Alberta went into their second lockdown. I had posted about following the rules, no matter how hard and frustrating it was. I tried to remind people other things can happen outside of Covid and that we can't be filling the hospital beds. I always thought of Colb. He didn't have Covid, but he needed doctors, ventilators, and a bed. And there was a shortage. Some people believed they wouldn't get Covid and believed if they did, it wouldn't be bad. But I was trying to remind others you can't prevent car accidents, brain tumors, and other illnesses so to please do whatever you could to help. You never wanted to be in a position where they had to pull your loved ones' resources to save someone else. I didn't think anything of it, other than just speaking from my experience and my heart. So, I posted it, and I went to bed. The next morning, I woke up to it all over the media. TMZ and New York Post headlines were "Colby Cave's widow lashes out against Covid deniers". I never wanted to post again. I felt anything I said or did was changed to fit whatever narrative the media was going for. It was debilitating. It was isolating. I had created an online community who was helping me and others, but I was constantly getting backlash. Plus, I didn't want to go anywhere outside because there were reminders everywhere I looked.

I remember a few widows talking to me shortly after Colb died. They were further along than me in their journeys and they warned me that it gets worse as time goes on especially around the one-year mark. They were right. It did get worse. Way worse. No one talks about this part of grief or trauma, especially on social media but I was trying to change that so no one suffered alone. Eventually, I hit a breaking point. Around the one-year mark of his passing, right after Colby's funeral. I shut down my social media. I posted this and shut it all down for a while.

"After receiving multiple fake accounts, commenting and messaging me extremely hurtful and inaccurate things for the last 12 months, and now even more so after Colb's service, I will be taking a break from sharing and posting. Being called things such as an attention-seeking whore, that my husband would be disappointed in me, that I am causing him so much anguish in Heaven, and so many other things, I have reached my breaking point, it has simply destroyed me. Colb would be broken for me. I am not in a good mental state as no young 27-year-old widow would be after many things that have been said and done. I can only take so much slander and mental and emotional abuse. I will not make it if it continues, I can say that confidently. I will not make it if this continues. Amazing family, friends, and therapy can only do so much. Lately, I'm petrified to look at my phone. I'm petrified to see what I will have been sent, or what people have said, or thrown at me, all while trying to grieve my husband, and being thrown in the public eye. In order to regain my confidence, and self-esteem, and wrap my head around many things, I need to protect myself, and to do that, I need to unfortunately, step away from something that has helped me with not just my grief, but many other people who are also grieving. I hope this won't be forever and I can come back but I need to have my cup "filled" before I can fill/ help others. Thank you to the 99% of people from all over who continue to love, support, and pray for me. It has kept me alive. I mean that I am alive because of so many of your guys' kindness, love, and support. Thank you will never do justice. It breaks my heart that I have to take a break from seeing all your love and support because of the 1% of mean people. However, I'm a human being with emotions, and sometimes it's really hard to ignore that 1% when it's constant and so incredibly personal. Please always be kind, you really never know what someone is going through behind the scenes."

I wish I could say as I am writing this, the cyber-bullying has stopped. But that would be a lie. It has slowed down, but I know it will pick up again after this book is published. I think I'm ready for it now. As ready as anyone can be. I know that I needed to tell this story for Colby and myself. I deserved that and so does he. Some people have this image and idea of what all went down. Some have written articles about what they think happened. And it was just important for me to get the true story out. Not other people's narratives. It was important to get the real story from the person closest to Colb. The person closest to the story. Me, Emily. Not just Colby Cave's widow, but Emily. The young woman that is still here today, living and breathing it all in. The good, the bad, and the ugly. One thing is for certain though, you will see it as you continue to read the rest of this book. I will not, ever again in my life, cover my pain to make others feel more comfortable. I will stand, share, and write with my gaping wounds, with my hands shaking, because if I am not vulnerable and honest about my PTSD, grief, and our love story, then I'm not doing Colb's story justice. He called me his "little world changer." World changers don't go quiet in times like these. They make a difference. They help others. So that is what I will continue to do in his honor.

CHAPTER 17

Chester

One thing is for sure, I am beyond thankful for Chester. He gets me out of bed each day. I mean that with every cell in my body. He's the last part of Colb I feel I have. Although we both have severe separation anxiety and we both still hope that Colb is going to walk through the door, we have continued to make him proud and have been through hell and back and back again. We both miss Colb so much and we can't wait to see him again.

I have this vivid memory of Chester a few months after Colb died. I was laying on the floor staring at a Ziploc baggy with a chunk of Colb's hair in it and I was crying uncontrollably. I remember thinking I just wanted to be held by Colb. I wanted him to tell me it was going to be okay. I wanted him to wipe away my tears and kiss me. This chunk of hair is the last physical thing I have of my husband, our dreams, and the future we planned together. We had cut a piece off when we went to say goodbye to his body. It's held together with a blue string that makes a bow. I don't just grieve my husband and best friend every second of the day. I grieve the daughter we dreamt of having, and how Colb was so excited to put her hair into a ponytail and tie it with a bow. I grieve the son we dreamt of having, and how Colb was so excited to teach him how to tie his skates just like his Daddy. I grieve the orphan we dreamt of adopting from Haiti, and how this child would have been such a beautiful addition to our family. As tears were streaming down my face, Chester came running into my bedroom, jumped onto my lap, put his two front paws around my neck, as if he was giving me a hug, and then started licking away all my tears. Chester knew what I needed in that moment. And he showed up for me. He still does. He does things like this all the time and I'm just so thankful to have him.

There were many nights I would go to bed and pray that I wouldn't wake up. But then my guilt would kick in and I realized that I couldn't do that to Chester. So, on the days that were harder than others. The ones that would bring me to my knees. The days when all I would want is for my heart to flatline, and it felt like I couldn't breathe for the life of me, I had to keep going for Chester and for Colb. I owed it to both of them.

They say dogs know more than we could ever imagine. I truly believe this now because I experience it every day with Chester. The months following Colby's death, Chester would not leave my side. I was petrified to leave him alone. Anywhere I'd go, he'd follow. And I never cared to leave him alone. Still to this day, I pay for a babysitter or someone to watch him, so he is never left alone. Some may think I am crazy, but I just can't stand the thought of him being lonely. This was amplified about 8 months after Colb died. After a scary and careless incident, I have never left Chester out of my sight unless he was in the care of someone I trusted. Chester ate something given to him that started to shut down his pancreas among other things. It was high in fatty acids. At first, I didn't think anything of it, but after a few days, it just didn't add up how sick he was. I thought he was going to die. I felt so guilty. It all started when Chester and I were out on our normal daily walk when I noticed his behavior really started to change drastically. By the time we got back to my place, Chester was foaming out of his mouth and having seizures. I frantically called my parents and sister back in BC and Ontario. I didn't know what to do. I froze. His regular vet was closed. The closest vet was 20 minutes away. My parents immediately called one of my close friends at the time who also lived in the building. He sprinted down to grab Chester and me. I remember him flying through the door and taking Chester from my arms. I was just in a daze and had flashbacks of all the confusion with Colb. Trauma has a way of doing that. I remember saying I needed a minute and that I was trying to find my phone charger. My friend started yelling, "Emily we have to go. We don't have time." We rushed to the emergency vet. Chester was foaming out of his mouth the whole time, shaking on my lap. We didn't think he was going to make it. When we finally pulled up to the vet, we couldn't go in because of Covid restrictions. I remember the nurse rushing out, grabbing Chester from my arms, and rushing into the facility. I was standing there in shock. One of the other nurses was trying to explain what was going on and it was all going way over my head. She asked me about signing a DNR (Do Not Resuscitate) or if I would give them permission to give Chester CPR. It brought me back to the phone call from the doctor before Colby went into surgery and me telling him, just do whatever he can to keep him alive. This time though, I couldn't respond. I could barely sign the CPR forms. My friend took over and had to sign them for me. I just couldn't believe what was happening.

We were eventually sent home and were greeted by two other friends upon our arrival. These three were my go-to people for a long time. Although they had never met Colb and only knew me as a new widow, they helped Chester and me greatly. I will always be grateful for that. They slept on my floor that night and we all waited for calls and updates from the vet. Chester would eventually be discharged from the hospital. He was put on a super strict diet to rebuild back his pancreas but was warned he will always have flare-ups now. It makes me sick to my stomach to think about it. All because someone carelessly gave him a piece of human food. And that's why I'll never leave him alone again. NEVER. The idea of something happening to him and him being the "last thing" I have of Colb, is unbearable. I understand that this is my grief and trauma, and it is something that I am working on day in and day out. Grief has a weird way of making an impact on different people in different ways. For me, my biggest thing, and hurdle still to this day, is Chester being left alone.

If you know Chester, whether you have met him quickly on the street, or are in our inner circle, you know he is not a normal dog. Whether he is sitting at the kitchen table watching us all eat. Saying hi to everyone as we walk through the airport. Sitting in his dog carrier like a baby on my chest watching people. He just loves to be around people. He is the happiest when he is around people and makes people so happy in return. This is exactly what Colb did too. He is such a light in our lives and continues to be.

I would not be here without Chester. Therapy has been extremely helpful, and the support of family and friends has been incredible. However, it's Chester that has been my little hero. My lifesaver. My saving grace. His curly red hair was just like Colb's. His big eyes. His human-like personality. My sidekick. My Chester, Chesty, Chestman. My mini Colb.

CHAPTER 18

The First Holidays

The holidays were always a big deal to us. Those were the few days off during the year when we got to spend time with each other with no hockey interruption. Not only did we get to celebrate Christmas, but the following day was Colby's birthday. Leading up to the first holiday season without Colby, I refused to celebrate it. I couldn't. The thought of setting up a Christmas tree without him and not hearing him tell me all the reasons he loved me after each ornament we put on, was far too painful to do alone. It was just so different that year. It was empty. At that time Covid was on the increase again and more stringent restrictions were being enforced. Due to these restrictions and Covid concerns, my sister and her family weren't able to travel to Edmonton to be with me and my parents. We were not supposed to see any friends outside of our 5-person cohort. After being alone for only a few months, my parents realized that they needed to move to Edmonton to be closer to me. I needed the support. Within three weeks they sold their home, packed it up, and moved across the country to make sure they would be there by Christmas. As I have said from the beginning, they are the unsung heroes in this story for all they have sacrificed to make sure I am okay.

It was a huge struggle coping with the fact that our first Christmas as a married couple was our last Christmas together. I wasn't looking forward to doing the holiday season alone. Knowing that everyone was going to wake up Christmas morning and still have their person was hard for me. I knew myself enough to know I needed a distraction, so I decided to do my best to fulfill the nickname that Colby gave him - his little world-changer. I told all my friends and family I didn't want any gifts and I didn't want to celebrate, so instead, I wanted anyone who was planning to spend a dime on me to spend that buying gifts for the less fortunate. Mainly, the children in the hospital and their families. So that's where I focused my time and my energy. My apartment was flooded with toys, pjs, and gift cards. We decided to host a pizza party for the inpatient children in the mental health unit. It was all so heartbreaking but so beautiful at the same time. The truth is, the remedy for me feeling so low was helping others. This began to fill my cup. I didn't need any gifts under the tree that year. The song, "Baby, all I want for Christmas is you" had a whole new meaning now. My focus became if I could bring a tiny bit of light and joy to others who were struggling and hurting then maybe the pain would be worth it.

I remember dropping off all the presents. We met the nurses outside of the hospital because of Covid. We loaded the boxes full of gifts onto trollies so they could roll them into the units. It was one of the many moments when I was feeling so broken but at the same time, I knew that Colb was proud. I would whisper to myself "For Colb". I am doing this for Colb. I am keeping his legacy alive. I am trying my best. Because if not with him then for him.

I went to sleep that night craving to just hold his hand. Colb had a habit of biting his nails and it drove me crazy and all I wanted was to be able to do was tell him to stop biting them. I would have done anything to feel his hand run through my hair. I would have done anything to look over and see his wedding band on his hand. It looked so damn good on his hand. I would have done anything to feel Colb squeeze my hand three more times. But instead, I was heading into Christmas Eve and Christmas day without him. Some of my people checked in with me and I appreciated that, but I knew they were all together with their loved ones and it made me so jealous and angry. I know I shouldn't have felt that way, but I did. They just didn't get it. Their cliche "thinking of you" stung. I knew they didn't know what else to say but it seemed like no one understood the pain I was in. The joy was sucked out of Christmas. How could there be joy when the joy of my life was taken away?

It was the first time in my life I was literally counting down the hours until Christmas would be over. But I also knew that the 26th was going to hurt just as bad. His birthday. His champagne birthday. His 26th birthday. There are 26 chapters in this book. I woke up the morning of the 26th feeling so empty. I just wanted to celebrate with Colby. I wanted to be with him. I felt like life had already been sucked out of me the day before and now I had to do it all over again. I didn't want ice cream cake. I didn't want to sing. I didn't want to do anything. I didn't feel a ton of hope for this day. But then I received a call from some of my friends inviting me to come out on my balcony patio and to look down into the parking lot. There I saw two of my closest friends Caitlyn and Joelle and some of Colby's teammates. Everyone was standing there holding massive signs saying how much they loved me. They had 26 balloons. They all started singing Happy Birthday to Colb as they released the 26 balloons up to the sky. Covid restrictions wouldn't allow us to be together (inside) but somehow this made me feel so loved and so close to them. It made me realize that I wasn't alone and that so many people were thinking of Colb and me that day. I sobbed and I asked them if I could come down and see them outside. I crossed the street and fell into their arms.

This is your friendly reminder encouraging you to show up for your friends. Yes, show up on their firsts. But continue to show up in the years following. There are always going to be more firsts. There are always going to be days that hit really hard. And just because some of the firsts are behind me, the seconds and thirds hurt badly as well. Remember the days. Not just the birthdays and the holidays, but also remember the "normal" days. I miss the normal days. Widowhood is lonely and having brief moments of not feeling alone is so special. I can't tell you how important it is to keep showing up for your people. You won't ever regret showing up. Even if it doesn't go the way you planned it to. Even if the person you showed up for is a complete mess and barely acknowledges your presence, it matters. It matters more than you could ever even imagine. I'm urging you to keep showing up. Because our people deserve to be celebrated not just on the big days, but on all the days.

One thing that shocked me during that holiday season was New Year's Eve being the hardest of all the days. I thought it would be Christmas or his birthday, but all the messages and kind gestures kept me a bit preoccupied. 2020 was the worst year of my life. It was hell on earth. No words will ever be able to describe what I had endured. The year my best friend and husband went to Heaven. The year I became a widow. The year we planned to have our first baby. Turned into the year I learned a new word that changed my whole life- colloid cyst. The year the word "inhumane" gained a whole new meaning to me. The year I deleted the list of baby stuff from my phone and instead made a reminder list of "death duties" that needed to be done. The year I learned how important it is to have wills, passwords, and joint bank accounts. The year I learned about cremation. The year I stood in a room filled with caskets. The year I picked out an urn. The year I gained "international spotlight" for the worst thing to ever happen to me. The year I learned the meaning behind the saying "you honor a man by the way you treat his widow." The year I saw the worst in many people but also saw the best in so many people. The year I continued to "live" when all I wanted to do was die.

2020, I hated you with every cell in my body. Everything was different now. Except for one thing, knowing how much my husband loves me, how proud my husband is of me, and how I am another day closer to seeing him. So many people were celebrating 2020 being over and ringing in the new year. But for me, the guilt I felt of "leaving Colb behind in 2020" was tragic. How could I move forward into a new year without him? How did people just expect me to move on with my life because of a stupid ball dropping from the sky in NYC? This wasn't a fairy tale like Cinderella. I wasn't dropping my glass slipper and my Prince Charming was coming after me. My Prince Charming had died. He wasn't coming to kiss me at midnight. I was here all alone. And whether I liked it or not, or how much I tried to fight it, 2021 was here and so was I.

There is something about widowhood and survivor's guilt that's undeniably hard to explain. I was carrying immense grief and guilt because I made it through 2020 and Colby didn't. I cannot help feeling every New Year to follow will be accompanied by a surge of survivor's guilt. Along with survivor guilt, there is also the painful realization that as time passes without Colb, the support continues to also fade away a little more each year. But what they don't realize is even as time passes, he's still the last thing I think about when I fall asleep and the first thing I think about when I wake up. I wish I could say it gets easier. The pain and sadness don't just go away. I grieve for Colby for every second, minute, hour, day, week, month, and year that we got to spend together. And also, for every second, minute, hour, day, week, month, and year we didn't get to have. I grieve for right now and everything going forward. I grieve that his life was taken away. I miss him today. I will miss him tomorrow. I will miss him 10 years from now and all the moments in between. I'll miss him with each New Year that comes my way.

Every time the stupid ball drops, I'll be reminded I'm heading into another year without my person. Without my Colb.

CHAPTER 19

Lover's Day

Colb was on a road trip for our last Valentine's Day together. Of course, I didn't know at the time it was going to be our last Valentine's Day, so I didn't think much of it. So instead of being able to spend the day with him, I went out with some of the Oilers' ladies, and he went out with some of his buddies in Florida. We had just been called back up in the NHL and one of my favorite stories about Colb's character went down that night. The pay difference between the NHL and the AHL is drastic. That night, even though he was out with his buddies who have big NHL contracts, Colb picked up the tab. I heard this story after Colby died from one of his best friends on the team- Ryan Nugent-Hopkins. As Ryan shared this story, he said how good of a guy Colb was and how he always showed up for people. His wife Bre and I had our bachelorette parties together. We got married just a few days apart. They were the first teammates Chester met. They were our people.

Though Colby and I weren't together on the exact day, he did send me flowers. The day he got back from his trip he brought me fresh flowers and surprised me with a beautiful gift and a nice dinner out. Colb never held back in expressing how much he loved me. He was so excited to celebrate our first Valentine's Day as a married couple. He had arranged for us to go out to a nice restaurant where he ordered a bottle of fine wine. He wanted it to be so special for us. Little did he know how special that memory will always be for me. The thing about Colb is he embraced every opportunity to live in the moment. It would not have mattered if it was a fine dining experience, a picnic on a beach, or going through a drive-thru, his big smile and loving gestures always made me feel special. That Valentine's dinner we didn't finish the bottle of wine, so we ended up taking it home. I didn't think much of it at the time. A few days later, we would get sent back down to California and this bottle would somehow be packed in our car at the rink in Edmonton. So when I moved back to Edmonton after Colby died, and we went to get the car from the rink, the bottle was still there. The half-drank bottle of wine from our last Valentine's Day together, months prior. I hid the bottle in the back of the kitchen cabinet when I moved into my new place, I couldn't even look at it without bursting into tears knowing I will never get another Valentine's Day with my husband.

Let me clarify something, I know nothing about alcohol. I like Prosecco and that is it. I am the girl who tells the waitress that I'd like a drink that doesn't taste like alcohol. I know nothing about wine. So before I share this next story, please remember this. I just thought the older the wine is, the better.

My first Valentine's Day without Colb was approaching and I wasn't excited about it in the slightest. I thought, in honor of Colb, I would pull out that special bottle of wine he had bought us. I would pour it into two glasses- one for Colb and one for myself. Since I have never been a person who knows much about wine, I didn't even think about the fact that red wine could go bad. I didn't realize that opening a bottle puts a timestamp on finishing it. The concept of an opened bottle of wine expiring never crossed my mind. I always heard wine gets better with age, right?! So, let's just say Colb was laughing at me from Heaven. I took one small sip and immediately spit it out in the sink. I proceeded to pour the remaining wine in the glasses back into the bottle and put the bottle back in my cabinet. I tried to cheers to Colb, but it was an epic fail in my eyes but Colb he would have burst into laughter.

I remember on my first Valentine's without Colb, some of our friends sent flowers on behalf of Colb. I remember the sweet card that said something along the lines of "Colby wanted you to have flowers today. He just needed a little help sending them." I remember the care packages that came from all over North America. Everyone was trying to make me feel so loved on Valentine's Day. I was so thankful for all of this. All the people who rallied around me saying, "we got you," "we're in this together," and "you will never be alone." They picked me up, held my hand, and helped me to stand when I couldn't do it on my own. I remember a follower of mine messaged me on Valentine's Day saying:

"Maybe the miracle was that he found you so quickly in his short life. Maybe that's your miracle. That he had so little time, yet he found you and loved you. And your continued strength, your continued journey of memories, and everything you're going to do for those kids with his Memorial Fund. They're miracles. Both his and yours."

Despite how hard it was to hear these things, I couldn't help but believe she was right. And it reminded me I would get through this day FOR COLB. I would remember all the love Colb gave me, even though I would do anything to have him back. I would do it for Colb. Everything I do, big and small, I do for Colb.

Shortly after Valentine's Day, the day that is supposed to be all about "love," I had to start the horrific task of planning Colb's funeral with the Oilers. A lot of thought went into this. It had been almost a year and Covid restrictions were still in place. The funeral we once thought Colb would have with thousands of people, and with Covid being over, wasn't going to happen anytime soon. We knew we needed to have a funeral. We needed a service because, without one, there is almost a denial that hangs over everyone. It is an important part of the grieving journey. I would often talk to my therapist about this. About how hard it was we didn't get to have a funeral for Colb right away. It felt like we couldn't have closure and so many people were longing for closure.

When deciding a date for the service, we came up with the one-year mark of his passing in April. We thought it would be a way for everyone to come together (virtually) to remember Colb. It was the best we could do in the worst of situations. So here I was, 10 months after Colb died, finally starting to plan a funeral, a few days after Valentine's Day. I don't know why I thought this, but I always felt that my "last duty" as his wife was to give him a proper funeral. Of course, this wasn't my last duty. But when it came to his death, it felt like an important part of the business side of it. And it was my duty. I needed this. Our family, our friends, and so many people needed this. We needed to all come together and remember Colb. So that's what we decided to do.

I went through both NHL schedules for the Oilers and Bruins. I picked a day when both teams were off. Unfortunately, with the NHL canceling some games and all the protocols, both teams ended up having to play the day of his service. However, they were able to watch it in the morning before their games. I thought of every little detail to make sure that everyone could be together virtually the best I could. Colby's family was the first to know about all the details. Weeks in advance, I asked his parents to speak. I also asked David Backes, Patrick Russell, and our pastor Josh to speak. Over the next few weeks, I found myself picking out flowers, lighting for the stage, curtains, and of course having to pick out a dress to wear to my husband's funeral. I became fixated on this. I wanted to look perfect. Not for the cameras and all the people watching but for

Colb. I wanted to look perfect in his eyes in the same way that I did for him at our wedding. Where he would look down from Heaven and say, "wow my wife is beautiful," just like he told me so many times at our wedding. We were only allowed to have 20 people in the rink for the funeral. There were still so many rules in place. The Covid restrictions were constantly changing. I wrote his eulogy. I wanted that to be perfect too. Just like my vows. One day, when I was talking to my therapist, I told her I received a text from Kelly Backes, talking about the funeral. She was checking in to see how I was doing. My therapist asked me what the text said, and I burst into tears trying to reread it to her. "Love you Em. Colby loves you. Chester loves you. So many people love you and see you in this."

It was happening. My husband's funeral. Almost a year after he died, I was finally going to have a funeral for him. My therapist asked me what I needed to make it through the next few weeks. She knew it was going to be very media-heavy, emotionally, mentally, and physically demanding. My answer was simple. I needed Colb. And I knew he'd show up. I was going to do everything in my power to make this day special in honor of him, no matter how painful it may have been for me.

CHAPTER 20

The One-Year Mark

Nothing can beat the pain of your loved ones' final days. What I didn't realize was how painful "reliving" those final days would be until the one-year mark of Colb's passing. I relived every last date. His last meal. Even down to the last time Colby cut his nails. I played them all over and over in my mind, I relived every single last thing. What did I miss? Were there any signs? What would I have done differently? I tortured myself leading up to his one-year mark. I relived every little detail, while trying to plan his funeral. I go back and forth with many emotions. Sometimes I would think I was grateful I had a year to process his death before planning his funeral, I was out of the shock, and I could put more attention to the details. However, on the flip side, having a year to think about it, and being out of shock, I felt a tremendous amount of pressure on every detail to make it perfect. Perfect for Colb. I knew cameras would be there. I knew so many people would be streaming and watching. There was a lot of pressure and a ton of emotions that came with this. I wasn't just planning a funeral, I was reliving our last days, and on top of that, I was finally starting to organize Colby's personal belongings I had carefully packed away right after he died. A lot of his things had been stored at his parent's farm over the years because we were always moving back and forth. However, like I said Colb loved to shop for clothes, shoes, and hats wherever we went. It was all those things that I unpacked and addressed.

I remember sorting his clothes. I packed up two containers for his family and I kept one container for myself and my family. Chester laid on his wedding suit and didn't want to budge. Colb wore a lot of suits, shirts, ties, jackets, and shoes for game days. These were by far the hardest articles of clothing to sort through. Holding his wedding suit which was engraved with our wedding date over his chest felt like being stung by a million bees all at once. Remembering our game day tradition that we started during the years of our long distance relationship, of me picking out his suit and then him sending me a picture before heading to the rink. A fun tradition that I would advise anyone to do. Even during the years we lived together, whether he was on the road or at home, he would still take a picture and send it to me. What I would give to be able to help him design or pick out a new suit. What I would give for just one more game day. Those traditions and silly routines are now treasured memories I will always hold close to. So please, take the time to make the silly rituals, make the traditions with your person.

To be honest, I didn't know how I was going to make it through the funeral. I was so stressed. I was feeling all alone and I had been incredibly hurt by those who I thought would also walk alongside me in my grief. Several days prior to the funeral I became super sick which would stress me out even more. I was so worried about coughing on stage and everyone thinking I had Covid and the entire world talking about it. Or even worse, testing positive and not being allowed into the rink. The list could go on. What we learned was I had been living in a condo with black mold in the ventilation ducts. Literally in my bedroom. My respiratory system was inflamed because of the mold. Though we knew I did not have

Covid, the fear of me coughing and people thinking that I did have Covid caused me additional stress. An added stress and fear because of a global pandemic. My immune system was crashing. I was trying every little thing to get better. Heck, have you ever drank boiled onions to get rid of a cough? I have. And it's disgusting. Oh, it also didn't work. So I'd recommend not trying it.

Roughly a week before Colb's funeral and his one-year mark, I had this overwhelming feeling I needed to make a call. Maybe it was reliving his final days and all the emotions that came with not being with him. Or maybe it was a year of working through my emotions. But one day I just decided I was going to call the head of critical care at Sunnybrook Hospital. And I did. I called his number. I remember feeling all the emotions I had when I was calling that same number for updates on Colb.

He didn't pick up. So I left a voicemail.

I told him that I was sorry for yelling at him on the phone when he told me I couldn't be with Colb. I told him I know they did everything that they could to save him. I told him about the funeral and invited him to watch it virtually. And then I thanked him

Honestly, I felt so good getting that off my chest. I never got a call back. I didn't expect one or even need one. I felt like I needed to say these things. I'm so glad I did.

My sister, brother-in-law, and little niece Sydnie weren't able to come to Colb's funeral. It was so hard not being able to have them with me at the funeral. But once again restrictions kept them on the island in BC.

I remember a few days before the funeral, I had a surprise visitor. My Mom ran into Dave Tippett, the Oilers' head coach in the elevator of my building. He asked how I was doing and my Mom was honest with him and just told him, "Not good." She then invited him over to see me. Technically, the team was supposed to be incredibly careful but at that moment, I'm not sure it mattered to him, he said yes. I remember him walking through the door, we hugged, and I just cried. I hadn't seen so many of our hockey people for so long. The NHL rules were so strict. Having one guy whom Colb and I loved so much, walk through the door meant so dang much. It took one quick conversation to remind me I am not alone despite how lonely it felt. Not long ago, I wrote a card to Dave and Wendy telling Dave the decision he made to walk through the door and give me a hug meant so much to me. One person. One hug. One conversation. It made all the difference in my world at that time.

The day before the rehearsal of the funeral I didn't know I'd even be able to muster enough courage to attend. Yes, we had to have a rehearsal for the funeral, as it was being streamed live, the music, the lights, the stage, and the walk-through, all had to be perfect. I felt like I was not ready and I couldn't do this. How was I supposed to read my best friend's and husband's eulogy? I was reliving our last days together. I was sick. At the same time, I had all this pressure on myself for it to be perfect. Rehearsal day ironically fell on "National Unicorn Day." Colb called me his Unicorn in his vows. I felt like it was his way of wrapping his arms around me from Heaven. I felt like he was telling me to keep on crawling, walking, or whatever it took to keep moving forward. To keep on living. To stay here. To stop, to sit, to breathe, and take it all in. I felt like he was reminding me he just got a head start getting to Heaven and he'd see me again soon. But he is not rushing me or any of us for that matter. He wanted me to continue to love life as he did and take advantage of each day.

I felt his presence reminding me. He was saying, "Em when the sun is out, go outside. When it rains, dance in it. When there's anything sweet to eat, eat it. And then eat some more. I felt that every double rainbow I saw was him sending me reminders of his love. Encouraging me to stop and admire the sunrises and sunsets. To be kind to everyone. To live in the moment just like he always told me to do. Pay for the person's order behind me and to brighten someone else's day. When there's someone to help, help them. Because life is precious." He showed me that. He showed me everything. He showed me love and how to love well. The purest and deepest form of it. He chose me. And I will always choose him. I can't wait to run and jump into his arms when I get to see him in Heaven. But for now, we celebrate him.

It took everything in me to carry Colb's urn into the rehearsal. I felt like I was carrying him into the rink for the last time. I remember gripping his urn as I walked through the long Zamboni entrance and hallway. I was about to turn onto the ice to see everything set up for the first time. Bob Nicholson was standing there with some of the other Oilers workers. Bob has been the backbone of keeping Colb's memorial fund going in Edmonton and putting his funeral together. He has done so much for me and my parents and continues to do so to this day. When I made eye contact with him for the first time, with Colbs urn in my hands, standing 6 feet away from him, I lost it. He wanted to be there to welcome me. To welcome Colb back to center ice. With tears flowing, I turned to see the massive jumbotron with Colby's face on it. The flowers. The stage. His jerseys. Our daily motto "be somebody that makes everybody feel like a somebody" on all the screens through the stands. I had only been in the rink on game days. But today, it was completely empty. And all of this was done for Colb. It was "perfect." I couldn't stop crying as I thought that he should be playing on this ice but instead, his ashes were on center ice. My Dad just held me as I cried on the stage. We did the run-through. We went through it all. And then we went home knowing that tomorrow was it.

I woke up that morning surrounded by so many of the people who meant the most to Colb and me. Colb's whole billet family was there. Of course, my parents were there. Matt and Loni (two of Colb's friends) and my friend Caitlyn were there too. They were all trying to encourage me the best they knew how. Today was the day. It was happening. My husband's funeral was finally happening. I remember putting on my dress and walking out of the room.

Everyone just stared at me and told me how beautiful I looked. I didn't feel beautiful, but it was nice to hear. In a strange way, it felt like when I put on my wedding dress. The hair. The makeup. At the same time, I still had the feeling that Colb could walk through the door at any minute. It has just been a year-long road trip, right?

I could barely walk to the rink. Both my parents were holding me. One on each side. I held onto Colb's urn so tightly. I hung out in one of the rooms with Loni and Caitlyn and read over my eulogy until right before the broadcast was going to start. Everyone was already seated. When I say everyone, I mean all 20 people that were allowed into the rink. And as I walked up to the front row and took my seat, I reminded myself, despite Colb being in Heaven, he was here. I forever have his love and that will always make me the luckiest girl in the whole world. There is nothing or no one that can ever take his love away from me. I feel it every single day, and as I walked up on that stage and took a deep breath. I knew he had my back.

And then I began to read.

"When Colb first died, I was so worried that he would be forgotten. I was worried that if we didn't have a funeral right away and waited too long that people would just move on. Standing here today, a whole year later, I can honestly say that is the farthest thing from the truth. Our family, friends, hockey community, and so many people all over have managed to rally around me and help me keep Colb's legacy alive. I don't believe thank you will ever do justice for all that has been done and continues to be done in honor of Colb. Somehow through my unbearable pain, I have felt so much love and encouragement. So, on behalf of Colb, and myself, I thank you all for being here with us virtually today.

For those of you that don't know how Colb and I met, let me share the story with you. It started 8 years ago, when Colb was playing for the Swift Current Broncos. He was sitting in the changing room and somehow came across my Instagram. He looked at one of his buddies and said, 'I am going to marry that girl one day.' We hadn't met, I was living in Ontario, I had no idea who he was, but he made up his mind that day that I was the one. It took me a little bit longer, maybe a year... actually almost two years... to finally 'Cave' to one of his many DMs. As soon as we started talking, I could tell he was really special, and I knew I had to meet him. So I mustered up all my courage and bought a plane ticket to visit him in Providence, Rhode Island. I will never forget him picking me up at Boston Logan airport. I was so nervous. As soon as he saw me walking out of arrivals, he quickly walked over with his big smile, grabbed my face, kissed me, and then told me 'I am gonna marry you one day.' I continued to play 'hard to get' over the weekend but I knew he was perfect, and as soon as I flew home, I told my family and all my friends that I had found my person, and Colb was right, I was going to marry him one day. Had I known that I would eventually become his widow just less than 9 months after our dreams came true of us getting married, and me becoming his wife, I would have only run faster down the aisle to him.

People ask me all the time, what is my favorite memory of Colb? It is so difficult to answer because when I think about us, I think about so many things. I think of the big things, like the day he kissed me for the first time at Boston Logan, the day we got engaged, the day Colb became a Christian, the day we got married and started our little family. I think about all our crazy moves and all our amazing vacations which usually resulted in him getting very sunburnt. I think about his first time meeting my family and my first time meeting his family. I think of all Colb's exciting hockey milestones- his first NHL game, his first NHL goal, and his Winter Classic at Notre Dame stadium. But mostly, I think about the intimate, quiet, and what I thought were the 'boring' moments. Memories I would have never held onto at that moment. Yet, I constantly find I replay them now. The things that happened every day, that no one else would see. I see Colb walking into our bedroom every time after coming home from a road trip with a big smile on his *face whether it was a win or a loss, how he would push my hair out of my face, kiss me, say that he missed me, even if I was half asleep. Him making all my favorite meals while dancing in the kitchen with nothing but his apron on. Getting all dressed up together for date nights. Movie nights on the couch, Colb loved pepper on his popcorn... or smarties. He sure had a sweet tooth... which would usually result in me telling him where the candy was hidden because he would give me his puppy dog eyes. On most movie nights, I would fall asleep within 15 minutes, he would be rubbing my ankles or playing with my hair. I would usually wake up with him carrying me to bed and tucking me in while he went to brush his teeth or turn off all the lights.*

We had a lot of car rides over the years that consisted of us singing our hearts out to different playlists depending on our mood or where we were going. Walking our puppy Chester, talking about how he would handle sharing the attention with a baby when we had one, and reading books about adopting an orphan from Haiti because it was something that I had wanted to do since I was a little girl. We planned our whole lives, all while thinking we were guaranteed all this time. Rolling over and kissing him good morning or goodnight, holding his hand and feeling him squeeze mine three times which was our way of saying "I love you" to one another, hearing his heartbeat as I lay on his chest. I remember each moment, hundreds of them. Me catching him smiling for no reason. Colb was always smiling. Whether it was a good day or a bad day, he always reminded me with that famous smile of his that all we ever needed in this crazy world was each other. I thought about why these seemingly small moments are so prevalent now. It's because those moments were when choosing Colb made all the sense. They were moments of pure content, protection, and complete love. If I could describe our love, that's how I would. I just knew I was going to be okay because I had him because he loved me.

With each year we spent together, our love flourished. We grew up together loving and living. Our love is the greatest love I've ever known and will ever know. Colb changed my life, he gave me a life that everyone deserves. He taught me to live a life worthwhile. He always put me first and I will forever be grateful for the happiness he brought me. I would give everything to have him here with me, and I think of him every second of the day. I know he is giving me the strength to keep going, even when I don't think I can. Colb lived life to the fullest and never took anything for granted, and even through his tragic death, he is a constant reminder to me and many others to continue to live life to the fullest. He has blessed so many people in ways that he will never know. Today, hug your husband or your wife. Tell them that you love them, and that you are proud of them. Annoy them. Take pictures and videos. Cherish every little moment.

Okay, here is the hard part, trying to end his eulogy. You know Colb could barely make it through the first word of his vows on our wedding day. You can hear him in our wedding video saying, 'pull yourself together man'. I remember joking and making fun of him after the ceremony. Although the roles are reversed most tragically, I know he's beaming down with pride but also making fun of me, telling me that I need to pull myself together.

Colb, my husband, soulmate, protector, and best friend, it breaks my heart but fills it at the same time -- watching the whole world see how incredible my husband was, not just as a hockey player but as a person. I am so proud of who you were, Colb, and will live the rest of my life hoping to make you just as proud. You called me your 'Little World Changer' and I promise I will fulfill that nickname you gave me by sharing our love story. I promise to continue to live our daily motto 'be somebody that makes everybody feel like a somebody'. I am so honored that you chose me to be your wife. It will always be the best title I was ever given. One thing I will miss the most is seeing you as a Dad. You would have been an incredible Dad. Being parents is something we talked about for years. We even picked out our baby names. I promise that we will care for so many kids together through your memorial fund. Those kids will be our kids, and our purpose together. You will guide, support, and love on them through me, from Heaven.

I was supposed to spend the rest of my life with you, Colb. But I now realize, you spent the rest of your life with me. I will always be honored that I was the one you loved till the day you went away. And will keep loving me, till the day we are together again. It will be the second-best day of my life, other than our wedding day. One day closer to seeing you in Heaven, babe, but until that day, I am so madly in love with you, Agape, my sweet angel hubby.

Forever and always,

Your number one fan, best friend, and wife".

CHAPTER 21

What Now?

Walking out of the rink after the funeral brought every emotion my way. Physically and emotionally, I had nothing left to give. I was spent. At the same time, my phone was blowing up from people all over the world that had watched on the live stream. Colby's family left right after the funeral to go back to Saskatchewan where all their family and friends would host a get-together. Before they left, we told them there were two bins filled with some of Colb's belongings that I had. Everyone knew that I was waiting until the one-year mark to go through his belongings because it was what my therapist had advised me to do. Looking back, I'm glad that I did that.

After the funeral, Caitlyn, Loni and Matt, Colby's billet family, and my family did their best to support me. We ordered pizza with a few of my other friends and tried to process all we had just gone through. The majority of the comments I saw about the funeral were really nice but as always, a handful of trolls showed up. This had become a pattern. It was always the same group of people. They would find any reason to attack me. What I said. What I wore. That I cried too much. That I didn't cry enough. My hair. My make-up. Anything they could find, they found.

The next day, Colby's Oilers' teammates would do a drive-by. They had signs saying how much they loved me and Colb and that they were thinking of me. A year later, they still couldn't even hug me so a drive-by was the best they could do. I immediately felt at the one-year mark, that the expectations of my grief and myself grew higher and higher. So many widows warned me about year two. They said it was different and almost worse in some ways. I didn't believe them. At least I didn't want to believe them. I will say, nothing is worse than the first days, weeks, and months after your partner dies. Trying to get through all the "firsts" is so hard. You constantly feel like you're drowning, you're suffocating, and just when you think you can breathe a bit, a tsunami hits you. Year one of widowhood is all about survival. But here's the thing with year two, it comes with just as much pain on so many days. Though the shock has worn off and you've climbed out of survival mode, the little things can put you right back into it. You planned to do your entire life with this person so you're always grieving moments you don't have with them. At the same time, people expect you to have a whole new life planned, move on, and be "over it" because it's been a year. Take a second and really think about that. Do you think you could have a whole new life planned within a year after losing your partner? It's like asking a baby who just learned to take a few steps to run a freaking marathon. It's insane. The judgment and the expectations that come with year two are ridiculous. At the same time, you almost feel a sense of abandonment from those who seem to just go on with their lives as if nothing happened. Yes, I made it through the first year, but there will always be new firsts that Colby was supposed to be here for. That will never change or will never go away. I felt so much pressure to "live for him and be happy." But let's be honest, that's just not realistic. I had a constant fear of my partner being forgotten and wanted to do all I could to keep his legacy alive. And if we are being honest, that's a load to carry. Each year without your partner brings a whole new set of emotions and challenges. Yes, the waves are different but when they hit, seemingly out of nowhere, you realize you can't swim like you thought you could.

A few days after the funeral Chester had to have surgery again. Extensive surgery. Multiple biopsies. His whole abdomen was cut open. I felt like I couldn't catch a break. When Chester was sick or puking after each surgery, I would just freeze. Even now when someone is puking, I freeze and don't know how to handle it. It takes me back to Colb that dreadful night and morning. I think this will always be something that makes me nervous and scares me. I think that's okay. I think it's okay that the flashbacks will always be there.

I never realized how badly I'd crash after the one-year mark and Colb's funeral. Many people think there is a deadline to grief. Your grief is allowed at the hospital, the funeral, and the following weeks, and if you're "lucky" some people will understand for the months following. But to some, after that first year, you should be all better. There comes a moment when people just expect you to move on. The "sorry for your loss" turns into judgment-like attention seeking. Your grief starts to matter less to people but to you, it all still feels the same. It's excruciating. It's complete and utter bull crap that grief has a time limit. We need to change the stigma around grief.

Some time had passed since the funeral, and I remember telling my therapist I was still madly in love with Colb and I knew I would always be. I knew I loved him the moment I met him and I will never understand why Colb was taken away from me. Or why our love story had to be the tragic one?

Colb changed my life. He gave me a life that everyone deserves. Colb was the epitome of love, happiness, and light. The funniest, smartest, most humble, best-looking person in the room, and incredibly kind even when people didn't deserve his kindness. There were countless times when people didn't deserve him, but he kept showing up. We were each other's number-one fan. We still are and always will be. I'm not just madly in love with Colb, but I'm also still protective over him and his legacy. That's marriage. That's Agape love. It never ends. No one dies if the love remains. It never goes away.

Colb's heart was too big for this place. I am so proud of who he was and will live the rest of my life hoping to make him just as proud. But I felt like so many people were expecting that to all go away. But what they didn't see is my emotions and feelings were still the same, no matter how much time passes. At the same time, some people did keep showing up, and those friendships and the sporadic check-ins mean more than anyone could ever imagine. You know who you are. I'm forever grateful to you for showing up for me. And for continuing to show up to this day. That being said, if you're still reading this, don't forget to keep showing up for your people. Just because time has gone by, it doesn't mean they don't need you anymore. To be honest, they may need you and your time now more than ever. So please, do me a favor, and check in on your people.

A few months after the funeral, I remember slowly starting to feel that I could breathe again. One day I even decided it was time to remove my wedding band and move my engagement ring to my right hand. It was a really hard thing to do, and I almost felt like I was cheating. But I also felt for some reason it was the next step for me. I just felt if I tried to keep them on my left hand, I would be in denial, and I didn't want to be there anymore. I found a lot of these moments were happening now. As time passed, things would hit me. I remember one day as I was getting ready to move into another apartment. A bunch of paperwork fell on the floor, and it was a bunch of Colb's medical paperwork. Among the papers was Colb's death certificate. It's crazy because it was the first time that I remember seeing it as my Dad had taken care of all the paperwork for me. I lost it. And then I went down a rabbit hole. I saw the name of the physician that called his time of death, and I immediately googled him. I then contacted my therapist livid when I couldn't find anything on him. My friend who was in her residency explained that residents and students often call the time of death. And that got me even more upset. What if they didn't try hard enough? What actually happened when Colb died? I wasn't able to be there, and I'll always have questions and concerns about what happened there. Three freaking words. Time of death. T.O.D. It rocked me to my core to see this. The moment you lose your best friend and the whole future you planned together with three effing words. Normally, you'd think of I love you but, in my case, and so many other widows it's the time of death or TOD. When I saw Colb's death certificate, I told my therapist I hated the man that called it. To be honest, I think I always will, and she said that is totally valid. He was there when my husband took his last breath, and I wasn't. He said the three words that officially changed my whole life in an instant. Grief and PTSD never end because the love never ends. Till the day I die, I will never understand why this happened. So please for all of us widows and widowers, go tell your person the best three words they could ever hear. I love you... RIGHT NOW before it's too late. You just never know. Please do it.

Another thing for me as time went on, and as the Covid restrictions started to lighten up was I became jealous and almost resentful. I felt angry about what I had been robbed of. I felt survivor's guilt I made it through the pandemic, but Colby didn't. There was finally a light at the end of the Covid tunnel and the world was opening up again.

A year still full of so many "firsts" and even though the shock began to slowly wear off, it was still excruciating. For me the second year of widowhood was almost as hard than the first in so many ways. It was the year I finally got to give my best friend the funeral he deserved (under the best circumstances I could.) The year I had the courage to stand on a stage at center ice, while people from all over the world watched me say my husband's eulogy. The year I started to really see his memorial fund and legacy come to life. The year I got to finally see more of our friends, family, and teammates for the first time since Colb died. It was a year in which I didn't just live 365 days, I fought hard battles every single one of those 365 days. Some I lost. Some I won. Some days joy and grief coexisted. The year I climbed my way out of rock bottom in order to continue to survive. Colb was gone and I was still here. Whether I wanted to be here or not, I was here. Now it was my time to figure out who Emily was. Not just Colby Cave's widow. It was time to find myself again. I just didn't know where to start.

CHAPTER 22

Boston: Our Forever Home

As soon as Covid restrictions began to lift, the first place I wanted to go was Boston. Boston was our forever home. It is where we planned to live even after hockey was over. It was the place I knew I would feel Colb the most. All of our best friends were there. As soon as the border opened up, I booked my flight back to Boston. Over the years, I always counted down the days until I was back in Boston. In the beginning, Boston meant I was going to visit Colb. Our first kiss was at Boston Logan. The butterflies and excitement were always high going there. The tears were always flowing leaving there as well. Eventually, Boston became my home with Colb. Our favorite place in the world. We planted our roots there. We made lifelong friendships and everlasting memories there. When Colb died, I wanted to run away to Boston because I felt like I would feel him with me there the most. This was not just a city we played for, but this was our home. I hadn't been back in almost two years, and I couldn't wait to be back "home."

Over that time, some of our friends had been traded and moved on. Some were now married or had babies. Some were still there. And although I have received endless love and support through technology since Colb died, there are no words to express what landing in Boston and being able to hug some of our people would feel like for me. I still caught myself thinking, Colb's there and I was flying to visit him. The hardest part of being a young widow in Covid had been watching everyone's life move on but feeling like I was at a standstill. So many people forget that even though Colb had been gone for over 16 months, I was still about to experience one of my biggest firsts- going HOME for the first time without Colb.

One of my best friends Kellie picked me up at the airport. This would be the FIRST TIME I saw her since Colby died. Think about that. Not being able to hug your best friend after your husband dies, until 16 months later. We went to the North End where I would try my first oyster for Colb. He always tried to encourage me to eat seafood, but I hated it. I can now say I absolutely love oysters. Every time I have one, I think of him. I spent a week in Boston and Providence. I saw some of our dearest friends and they loved on me so well. We cried a ton. We laughed a ton. I finally felt at home again and I belonged here. I was the happiest I had been since Colb died. I felt safe. I felt Colb.

You see, some people think that your family is blood. However, for Colb and myself, our family wasn't just blood. Our friends were also family because we were always so far away from ours. They were such a big blessing over the years and continue to be. That trip brought back some of the sweetest memories. I visited some of our favorite places. I walked Newbury Street and went into Colb's favorite stores. I went to Tatte Bakery and Monica's in the North End with my hockey sister, Bradley where we had a big glass of Prosecco for Colb. I walked around our old neighborhood and burst into tears when I saw the Whole Foods that we would go to together. I went to Mike's Pastry and got our favorite type of cannoli. I ate it standing in front of TD Garden, all by myself. I didn't have the courage to go in. I thought I may never be able to do that again. I didn't think I was ready. But little did I know, less than two months later, I wouldn't just be walking into TD Garden, I would stand on center ice, and I'd be doing the ceremonial puck drop for the Bruins' vs Oilers' game in Colb's honor.

Two months later, I flew back to Boston again with my parents. This was the first game since Colb died when his two teams would play against one another. I remember landing to the most beautiful sunset and feeling like Colb was welcoming us home. The entire Bruins organization went above and beyond that week to honor Colb so well. The day before the game I went to the Bruins practice facility to see some of his teammates and coaches. Mind you, I hadn't seen any of them since Colb died. I was met with so many hugs and so many tears. I had waited for this moment for so long. To be able to see his brothers after all this time meant so much to me. I always say I feel Colb the most when I'm around his teammates. His brothers. They knew him best. I was so happy to get to be with them. I could tell a hundred stories from that day. All so special and beautiful to me. I not only got to see our Boston teammates but also our Oilers family. It was as close to perfect as a day could be since Colb died. I felt him everywhere.

I woke up the next day feeling as nervous as our wedding day! Many people don't realize that I'm an introvert. Colb was the outgoing one. I don't like the eyes and the attention on me. It gives me anxiety. I had to interview with SportsNet before the game that evening and I remember saying this to the host Gene Principe:

"I was talking to someone about when I watched Colb play his first NHL game. I watched him at this center ice, and I thought I was so proud of him then. At TD Garden, watching him play his first NHL game. Going on the ice tonight, and dropping the puck, where he played his first NHL game. I never imagined I would be doing this years later. But I am even more proud of him, and his legacy. I always cheered him on at the Garden, and Rogers Place, but I was texting his teammates

last night and this morning. Colb's gonna have the best seats at the Garden tonight. He's front row in Heaven with his big famous smile on his face. He is probably making a joke about me not slipping on the ice. But as proud of him as I was when I watched him play his first NHL game here, I didn't think I could be any more proud but I am a trillion times more proud if that is possible, and I didn't even know that was possible."

Before the game started, I was waiting by the bench when they began playing a memorial video of Colb on the jumbotron. I was so nervous the moment it ended, and I stepped on the ice. The entire place gave me a standing ovation and all I could think of was, "Don't slip Em, don't you dare slip." Looking up into the stands and seeing everyone that loved Colb so well was so good for my heart. They were all there to honor him. And at that moment I remembered something my therapist would often say to me:

"Because even on your worst days, in your hardest times, you're still a million times stronger than so many people could ever imagine you have to be."

For Colb. I was doing it all for Colb. Colb's legacy is heart-wrenching and beautiful, and I had promised to devote everything I had left in me to continue it and to make him proud. Despite Colb not physically being here with me anymore, it doesn't mean that he is not helping me and giving me the strength to continue to be open, inspire, love, and help people. So, as I was standing on that ice about to drop the puck, I made my vow once again to him. The same vow I made privately alone in the hospital room. I am keeping it. Because it is my honor to continue to spread his light and love. To continue to try and be his little world changer.

I hugged every single Bruins teammate as I walked off the ice. I thanked them for their continued love and support. Told so many of them Colb loves them so much. Thanked them for being right beside me, sometimes carrying me, and helping me honor his legacy.

The following day I headed to Providence to meet with Hasbro Children's Hospital to discuss ideas of what we'd like to see happen with the memorial fund. I attended the Providence Bruins game that evening and did the puck drop there as well. Colb and I had so many great memories in Providence and probably spent more time there than anywhere else. And though most of the teammates that we played with were gone, I still felt so much love and support from that community. When the week came to an end, I didn't want to leave. I wanted to stay. As I said, I felt at home here in Boston. All our people were here. I felt Colb the most here. But the only thing that got me back on that plane to Edmonton was knowing Chester was there and I was ready to get back to him, my little piece of Colb who was still here with me.

CHAPTER 23

Signs From Heaven

Right after Colb died, my friend Carli Skaggs, the first widow friend I made, sent me a book called Signs. I'd been told by many people Colb would find unique ways to communicate with me from Heaven or give me signs to show his love for me. To be honest, I didn't believe it but at the same time, I hoped it was true. I remember reading the book and not being "open" to signs from Heaven in the beginning. But at the end of the book, there was a story of a loved one who also did three hand squeezes like Colby and I did. I had never heard of anyone doing this before. I remember thinking that was Colby's way of saying he felt those three hand squeezes through the nurse as he was taking his last breaths. It brought me some sense of weird comfort. After reading the book, I started writing down every little or big sign when I felt Colb's presence. I still have the book and I still add things to it often. I encourage anyone who has lost someone to do this. It is so special to look back and see over time. It's amazing how often our loved ones in Heaven show up for us.

One of the biggest signs Colb sends me is double rainbows. The months after Colb died, people in Edmonton who lived here for their whole lives said that they had never seen so many double rainbows. They would happen on the days when I needed them the most. When I needed a reminder. Big days where I had something hard to do. Birthdays. Anniversaries. Game days. The list goes on and on.

Another sign that happens on some of those special days, is the unopened bottle of Prosecco that I have on my counter or wherever I put it, pops and opens by itself. I know it sounds crazy, but it is true. I don't know how it is possible, but it has happened a handful of times where the cork just goes shooting up to the sky and bubbles over without anyone near it or touching it. I feel like it is Colby's way of celebrating me on certain days from Heaven. Opening the bottles for me like he used to in person.

I remember one time being on the phone with a reporter about the release of our song "Agape". I had just pulled out a unicorn stuffed animal that Colby bought me a few years earlier. I was fiddling with it as I was on the phone, and I noticed that something was written on the tag. As I looked closer, in faded ink, it said Agape. I had no idea that Colb had written that on the tag, but it was perfect timing.

On days when I needed encouragement the most, I would find random packages at my door. I remember one time in the fall when I was really struggling. I hadn't showered in days, and I didn't want to. That day, the Irwins, Chantel, and Matt, the first hockey couple we met in Providence, sent me a huge self-care package. Or when Julie and Danton Heinen, two of our best friends, sent me a gift card to book flights to get away from all the painful reminders in Edmonton. It is in these moments when I feel like it is Colb working through other people to encourage me and spoil me.

On top of all that, one of the biggest things is I feel Colb is in my dreams. I have had a few extremely vivid visitation dreams where Colby has come to talk to me about different things. The first one startled me so much that I woke up. I thought he was at the end of my bed. Chester was barking and I felt his presence. He told me I did all I could do as his wife and he was proud of me and some people never change and it is okay to walk away and let it all go to protect myself. It sounded exactly like him. He was crying. He felt so bad. Weeks later, what Colb was hinting at in that dream would all come true. It was like he was trying to warn me. Unless you have experienced a visitation dream, they are extremely hard to explain. You don't want to fall back asleep because they seem so real. It keeps you longing for more and more.

One of the most heart-wrenching but also super important visitation dreams would come in the fall of 2021. Colb showed up and encouraged me to start dating again. He not only gave me permission, but he said he was rooting me on. And no matter how much I tried to push that away as I wasn't ready for it, I would eventually have the courage to listen to the sign... just a little bit... just a baby step.

CHAPTER 24

If You Are The One She Lets In

This chapter comes with a lot of emotions. It was one of the hardest but most hopeful chapters for me to write. It took a long time for me to be "ready" to share this chapter because the truth is I warred with myself, the horrific survivor's guilt that comes with young widowhood, and the fact that Colb is gone and I'm still here. I think back on a note that was left outside Rogers Place after Colby died. Oilers' fans left flowers, notes, stuffed animals, etc., as the rink lit up saying "Rest in Peace Colby." It was from a young fan, and it said:

"I remember your wife reading to me in school and I am going to pray for her to be happy again."

During the season, the Oilers' girlfriends and wives would go into schools to read to students during their reading weeks. When I saw the note at that time, I remember thinking there was no possible way I could ever be happy again. Nor did I want to.

Being in the public eye, I had so much judgment on who and when I should date again. When Colby was still alive in a coma, I had people write I should just go out and cheat on him because he was not going to make it anyways. Within days of his death, I had people tell me he would want me to be happy and I needed to move on because he was not coming back. When I continued to post about Colby and my grief journey, months and even a year after his passing, the judgment only got worse. As I mentioned earlier, the cyber-bullying got so bad I had to deactivate my social media after his funeral.

I was darned if I did, and darned if I didn't. If I didn't post about Colby then I was moving on and if I did then I was stuck in my grief. People forget that because of the pandemic, my grief was extremely delayed, and I was living alone in isolation the majority of the time. So why would I ever want to date and bring someone into this mess? I started to believe I was "too widowed and broken" to ever be loved again.

I began to talk with some of my widow friends about dating. Some had been dating for a while. Some hadn't started yet. We talked about the pros and cons of both. I didn't feel comfortable talking to anyone else because I knew they wouldn't get it. I am sure you can tell by now that my family and friends are awesome but unless you have been in this position, you can't possibly get it. No one could fully prepare me or convince me that I was "ready" to date again. At times I didn't know I would ever be ready. However, after some time I began to feel my heart was beginning to open up to the idea of dating again. No matter how hard I tried to fight it, I also began to understand deep down there was going to be a new chapter for me. A chapter I never wanted but had been given. A chapter no one could have prepared me for. A chapter that would have me learning to love again, all while still being in love with Colb.

Before I share a few pivoting moments that got me to the point of being ready to date again, I hope you can take some advice or parts of my story to help a widow or widower you may have in your life. As I have said a few times now, I was petrified to date again because I had convinced myself I was "too widowed." I also convinced myself if I dated again then people would think I love Colb less and was over him. But I want to make something very clear. I'm still in love with Colb. I always will be. I never wanted to do life without him. This journey hasn't been easy, and there have been multiple people who have helped pave the way and supported me for this to be possible to share openly. Me being open to dating does not make me love Colb less. Not a day goes by when I do not think of him and my love for him will never go away. He is still very much present. He will be forever because he owns half of my heart.

Moment #1: It was a few weeks after Colb's funeral when I went out for dinner with some of the Oilers' girls for the first time in what seemed like forever. We ended the night at Lauren and Connor's house. When we got there, we were talking about a bunch of things, and I don't remember exactly how the conversation about my dating life started but it did. The conversation I had dreaded happening, was happening. I felt so uncomfortable. I felt like I was talking about cheating on Colby. Then Connor said, "I miss Caver, but he would want you to date and love again. We all want you to date and love again. We support you and are here for you when you're ready." This is something I heard so many times, but I hadn't heard it yet from the right people - the people that I knew missed and loved Colby so much. With one sentence, I felt like some of the weight had been lifted off my shoulders and they wouldn't judge me for trying to date again. Looking back, I was worried about people's judgments on dating because the trolls were constantly at me, but I think deep down I was actually more worried about hurting our family and friends by dating again.

Moment #2: It was the end of the summer, and I still wasn't in a great space with the whole dating thing. One day, I had my Spotify playing as I was cleaning my apartment, and a song called, "If You Love Her" by Forest Blakk came on. It hit me hard. I immediately googled the lyrics. It is supposed to be a cute love song but when I listened to it, I heard Colb saying these exact lyrics to the possible man I may date in the future. After reading the lyrics over and over again, I found a weird sense of peace in them:

"Take it
If she gives you her heart
Don't you break it
Let your arms be a place
She feels safe in
She's the best thing that you'll ever have
She'll love you
If you love her
On days when
It feels like the whole
World might cave in
Stand side by side
And you'll make it
She's the best thing that you'll ever have
She'll love you
If you love her like that"

These lyrics lit a hopeful flame in me. I told myself when I go public for the first time dating again, I would somehow incorporate this song because this is exactly what Colby would say if he could sit him down and talk to him. I just didn't know who this "him" was yet.

Moment #3: Not long after hearing this song, I had a conversation with my sister, Ky, and my brother-in-law, Dave about dating. We were on FaceTime and Dave said something that has stuck with me to this day. He said, "Colby would want you to be with someone he would joke about and be glad you didn't meet him earlier or you may have never married him." It set the standards high for me. "Date someone Colby would be proud and happy that you are dating."

About 7 months after Connor made his initial comment to me and I felt I had my first pivoting moment regarding dating, I felt like I was hitting rock bottom. I was tired of feeling so alone. I texted one of my friends, explaining that I was exhausted living without Colb. I wanted all the pain to end. I was having a lot of visitation dreams from Colb leading up to that point but that night, I had one of the most vivid dreams I have had since his passing. This was the last visitation dream I've experienced. It happened in November 2021. I have mixed emotions looking back on this dream. It still feels so real. I was in the fetal position on a hospital hallway floor and Colby was holding me. He was glowing. I was sobbing and begging him to let me die. I told him I was so tired, and to please take me with him. I didn't want to live anymore. To be honest, it didn't feel like a dream. It felt like he was right there with me so much it still startles me to think back on it. He was telling me it is going to get better and I needed to stay because it wasn't my time yet. I continued to sob and begged him to let me die and he just continued to assure me that my time wasn't done here yet. I remember waking up and trying to fall back asleep so I could see him more. That whole day I felt like I had just talked to, seen, and hugged Colb in person. It was comforting but heartbreaking. That night, I went to bed again and prayed that he would come back to me in my sleep to talk to me more. As I was laying there trying to fall asleep, I said out loud…

"Okay Colb, if you want me to stay here on Earth, you better send me someone really soon or I am not going to make it here much longer."

Two weeks later, he did.
His name is Colin.
And he was sent straight from Heaven.

CHAPTER 25

Colin

It started with him making one sassy comment about watching Selling Sunset alone and now here we are.

Colin's chapter.

Colin was living in Seattle at the time, and I was still in Edmonton. After our first FaceTime, which was almost 5 hours long, I texted my best friends and sister saying that "Colby would be impressed." I knew when I hung up that Colin was my answered prayer. And for the first time since Colby died, I felt such a calming peace. It was on that FaceTime, with his kind smile, Colin told me, "I am not going anywhere." And he said that after spending hours listening to me talk about Colby. Something I never thought was possible. I was unwillingly dragged into a fire, but I never imagined someone would be willing to step right into the fire with me. Colin has done just that. Our story isn't a traditional one, yet he came into my life at exactly the right time. When I still didn't think I was ready, but I needed his love the most. He found parts of me I didn't know existed, and in him, I found a love I no longer believed was real.

One story that sticks out in the first few weeks of talking with Colin was when we were FaceTiming on Christmas night. Colby's birthday was the next day, when midnight struck, we were still talking, and Colin, without any hesitation said, "Happy Birthday Colby." I remember feeling a wave of emotions. It almost felt too good to be true. Maybe it was possible to have both?

My original plan to fly to Seattle to visit friends quickly got bumped up by a few weeks. I spent a week in Seattle. A week that completely changed everything. A week when my head finally lifted above the waters and showed me that Colby was right in my dream and things were going to get better. Within 7 days, it was confirmed that this relationship doesn't take away the loss, trauma, pain, or love of Colby. It doesn't make Colin second best either because I could never compare the two. Colin has given me a refreshing confidence, hope, and gift I never thought was possible after Colby died. With Colin, my life has been filled with so much joy again, and at the same time, he has helped my fears go away. He has taught me that in the darkness, in the chaos, in the despair, and in the grief, love is always possible.

That week, Colin and I went to dinner with Bradley and Ryan Donato. Two of our close friends that Colb played with in Boston. I remember being so nervous, but I didn't want Colin to know so I tried to play it cool. It was a big deal to introduce him into this world and for them to be the first two people he met. The dinner went better than I could have imagined. Colin fit in perfectly. It was also during that week I met his three siblings and one of his cousins. I was so stinking nervous but again it went better than I could have imagined. It actually went so well I was invited back a few days later for a sibling weekend up at the cabin. Meeting Colin's family was a big deal for me. I was worried about them judging the history of Colby. The fact I was in the public eye, and possibly being worried about Colin feeling second best. I could go on. But just like Colin, they accepted and respected my past too. One of the most beautiful gifts I think someone can give to another person. When I went to bed that night, I remember thinking again, it almost felt too good to be true. Then I woke up to a text message from his sister-in-law, Mary, and it confirmed to me not only was Colin Heaven sent, but his family was too. Here are parts of her text:

"What happened to Colb is unimaginable and unbearable. I cannot believe the strength you have shown as a human to be where you are today. There is no denying that and the love that you just show on your feed for him is infectious. You should never ever downplay that because he's a part of you, a part of your soul, and a very important part of your life story. Colb was taken from you way too soon and I cannot imagine the pain you have been through. I can't believe the courage you have every day to wake up and take on the world, to be Chester's mom, and to carry on Colby's legacy. But not even knowing him, I know from what I've heard and seen and read this; he loved you. He would want you happy, and he will continue to live on through you. You have already shown so much in remembering his legacy through what you do for the NHL. I would never want Colin to replace him or try to. But what I can say is that I would be so excited to see him be a part of your next chapter. And Colin never has to be a replacement, nor a reason you can't still love Colb. Rather, it's a new chapter that I hope brings you joy. A chapter you never imagined for yourself, but hopefully a chapter that is just what you needed. —Colin also has the heart to know you should never stop loving Colb and that he knows there are chapters in life here. So please don't ever think you're making him feel like second fiddle. And I don't think the Boit clan will ever think that too. I've been waiting 10 years literally to see him smile like he did tonight. As for the public eye stuff- none of that stuff matters in the end what matters to us is how happy you are and how happy Colin is. This family is strong and tight knit and they will always protect you both. So don't ever let that keep you from being happy. It's a part of you, a part of your story, and you should never be worried about that."

You can imagine the tears FLOWING after receiving that text. I flew home for a few days, packed my bags, grabbed Chester, and then flew back for sibling weekend at the cabin. Everything was going amazing until I had to test for Covid to fly back to Canada. Of course, I tested positive and so did Colin. So, we had to quarantine together for 18 days (with Chester). Let me tell you if that's not a way to start a relationship, I don't know what is!

At this point, I wasn't ready for many people to know about Colin. It's not that I didn't want to tell the world, I was just afraid of what the world would say. I didn't want Colin to get backlash and I just wanted to keep it a secret before any negativity could ruin what we had. After the 18 days were up, Colin flew back to Edmonton with me for the first time to meet my parents and some of our hockey friends. I remember Colin saying something to me before dinner to meet Colby's teammates. He said, "I know I wouldn't be here if Colb didn't die. I am so grateful that I get to share you with him." He knows and has continually accepted my grief from day one. There has been no judgment from him with me "still grieving." There is no jealousy. There is no drama. He gets it. He has seen not just me cry but during his first trip to Edmonton, family and friends crying and talking about Colb too. He went to a hockey game and a Colby's Kids' skating session. He jumped right into the life and the job I have here in Edmonton, honoring Colb. However, he didn't look at me as "Colby Cave's widow" instead, he just looked at me as Em. My reply to him was very simple, "Colb is looking down, seeing all the kids his memorial fund is helping, seeing how supportive you are, and he's okay with it." I know Colb would be okay with it because that's the type of guy he was. I just wish they had a chance to meet each other because I know they would have been friends. It was after that trip that I went for it.

I shared with the world in an Instagram reel, using the song "If You Love Her" by Forest Blakk, that I was dating Colin. My phone blew up. Colin's phone blew up. It was A LOT. The "band-aid" had been ripped off. I don't think I could ever describe all the emotions a widow goes through when publicly announcing they are dating again. The survivor's guilt and the excitement at the same time. Some days, I wonder if I will always have both. It is nothing against Colin. It is nothing against Colb. You can never compare the two. I never want either of them to feel second best and every single day I have strived to show that to not just both of them, but also to Colin's family and friends as well.

Although, 99% of the comments and messages were positive when I first posted about me dating again. The 1% of negative ones stung and didn't make the survivor's guilt any easier.

"Do you truly miss your husband? While you're in bed with another guy"

"Colb would be disgusted with you that you are dating again. Rot in hell."

"With all due respect, I remember a time when I felt your pain, I cried with you, for you and Colb. But now things are different, you are with another man. You can't have it all. Widows pain, saying you miss your husband in Heaven, and post pictures with your new man. It doesn't make sense to me, and I am sure many others. What if you were Colb? How would you see it from up there? THINK."

"So, is the trick to get an ugly athlete to marry you and then pray he dies? Then wait for a few and start dating a new guy?"

Although the negative ones have calmed down a bit, they still sting to read when I get them here and there. I know they will probably increase after this book is published and I have accepted that. I have a better grasp on my survivor's guilt now, but it is something that I know I will never fully heal from. It will always be a part of me and something I will work on until my dying day. That is just a part of being a young widow who has fallen in love again.

The first few months of Colin and my relationship were a whirlwind but in a good way.

I always say to Colin I feel like I am a better girlfriend for losing Colb. I have learned to not sweat the small stuff. I have learned we only have one shot at this life, and we must give it our all and love hard.

Dating a widow isn't easy. Not only isn't easy for the widow, obviously, but stepping into those shoes is a lot to ask out of anyone. I remember when Colin came to Boston for Colb's two-year mark. The Providence Bruins were retiring his number. The first player in Providence Bruins history to ever have their number retired. Colin came without any hesitation. Not only was he there, but one of his best friends from college flew in as well. The emotions were super high. They watched me and some of our closest family and friends cry. Yet, they still loved on us. They supported us. I feel like it shows so much about both their characters. A few weeks after that game, I went to Arizona to visit Colin and his family.

Quick backstory. A week before Colb died, he loaded up my Starbucks' card. We used it in the airport before flying back to Canada. I hadn't touched it in over two years. It had $7.84 on it. I told myself I would never use it because I felt like it was Colb officially buying me my last tea latte. On that trip to Arizona, two things happened that would be pivoting moments. After a lunch date, we had with Wendy Tippett and a few other hockey girls to meet Colin, we ran to the grocery store and Starbucks. It was at that Starbucks where the barista would accidentally use the card that Colb had loaded for me. I started crying in the middle of the grocery store. Colin put two and two together and knew exactly what had happened. The card had accidentally been used. I remember handing him his coffee and saying that Colb bought us our Starbucks that day. He bought my new boyfriend Starbucks. Kinda twisted right? But here is the thing, although some tears were shed, it wasn't AS PAINFUL as I thought it was going to be.

I survived it. It was at this moment, I realized that no matter the future, doing the hard grief things, I would still survive, especially in this new chapter of dating again.

Another moment I had during the trip was with Colin's Dad, Peter. They had some family over one night and their Aunt who didn't know my backstory asked how we met. When I brought up having friends on the Seattle Kraken because of Colb, she proceeded to ask, "Who's Colb?" I was stunned. I didn't know how to respond. I didn't want anyone to feel uncomfortable. But I proceeded to tell the story of Colb, and they were all so supportive and understanding. After a pretty lengthy discussion, I walked into the kitchen and apologized to Peter for not knowing what to say and how to discuss it all. His response was perfect. He told me that when people ask about Colin's girlfriend, they just say that I'm from Canada and tell people what I do. He explained it wasn't their place to bring up Colb. Not because they weren't supportive of him but because to them, I was Emily. I wasn't Colby Cave's widow. I was my own person. I felt like someone was looking at me as my own person for the first time in a long time. At that moment, I felt like I finally had my own identity.

Colin and I spent the next few months traveling before he started business school. Something I was excited about because, with Colby's career, we were never able to travel a ton. Colin eventually started school at Wharton in Philadelphia. This was in August of 2022 and that's about the same time I decided I wanted to write this book. I remember talking to him about it and worrying about how this book will impact him. I worried about the trolls. I worried about his family and friends. I love Colb. I always will. However, I also love Colin. It is a hard journey, but it is rewarding. As I said, I am privileged enough to not be able to love once but to love twice.

During the first few weeks of Colin being at school, we both ended up getting sick from mold exposure. So sick we ended up having to go to the hospital. I will never forget them triaging us in the emergency room. I was in worse condition with bronchitis than he was, so they separated us. I panicked. Watching him go through a separate door from me wasn't fun. There is a ton of PTSD still there. I didn't know what the doctors were doing to him, and I was so scared. I texted both our parents and Colin in a full-out panic attack. I couldn't breathe. I was in a hospital room all alone. And so was Colin. My heart rate was incredibly high, and they couldn't get it down. It triggered something in me, I don't think any words can explain the way I was feeling. The idea of Colin being out of my sight and in a hospital even though it wasn't remotely like Colby rocked me to the core. We obviously came out of that situation okay but my reaction to it all wasn't good. I ended up telling my therapist I felt like all the work that I had put into triggers and PTSD had all been washed away. I felt like I was a failure and back to square one. I think that is the thing about PTSD. It's something I will probably have for the rest of my life. I will always have anxiety, especially around illness or death. And that is OK. It is OK to still have those moments. I am human. I have been through hell and back. Even though I have made a lot of progress, I've still got a long way to go.

As the book started to come to life, I remember having a discussion with Brandon, one of my closest widower friends. He has been a constant encourager for me. He has 3 little kids and I texted him asking as a parent how he would feel if he were one of Colin's loved ones reading the book and he replied with this…

"I'd be like, don't let this one go. Don't screw it up. This one loves so well. She loves so well that when she lost the person she loved the most, she made a vow to keep his memory alive and is doing just that. I'd tell him that he doesn't ever have to worry about the way this person will love him. That she will always show up for him. That this person means what she says and will follow through on her commitments. That he'd be crazy not to be just as committed to her. Because most chicks suck. And this one doesn't. Don't screw it up, kid."

I am not saying by any means Colin's loved ones have given me any form of doubt and Colin sure hasn't. It has been the complete opposite actually. But I wanted to share this because yes, the book is For Colb, but the ending of this book would be different if it wasn't for Colin. If it wasn't for his love, support, and understanding I wouldn't be in the place I am. And although, you never exactly know what the future holds, even though I have a good feeling about him, I wanted my readers and other fellow widows to know it is okay to still have survivor's guilt. It is okay to love two people. And if anyone, I mean anyone, judges you for that, or gets jealous, they don't deserve you. Because as Brandon shared with me, we love so well. And you'd be lucky to have us.

CHAPTER 26

His Little World Changer

"How are you doing now?" I always reply, "it comes in waves."
There will be days when the waves of grief hit you and you're thrown right back to the very moment you lost your person. You will probably doubt if you're strong enough to keep going and wonder if all the work you've done in therapy has actually helped you at all. When they do hit, I try to remember that these waves are so intense because the love is still intense. They don't have to set you back. They remind you how precious life can be and how far you've come. They remind you nothing in this life is guaranteed. They remind me how lucky I was to have Colby in my life. I have learned to hold onto the waves of grief now instead of trying to fight them.

Looking back on the last 3 years, as hard as things have been, I have felt so much love and encouragement. I know what it feels like to not want to live, but at the same time, I am thrilled I get to be here. Because I lost Colb, I now strive to live a life that inspires others. Grieving or not, I just want to live a life that inspires others to live and love better. I fought, and continue to fight, long and hard, to get to the place where I am today. I don't ever want to be scared to share the vulnerable and dark moments because what terrifies me more is someone feeling alone or judged while walking in their grief. As I continue to share my journey, I will always think of Colb. Every single time I get up on a stage. Every single time I hit share on a post. Every single time I talk with someone about their grief. Every single page of this book. Every single day. He made me into the person I am today. I have this platform for the worst possible reason and if I went quiet in my grief or shut people out or got angry, I wouldn't be the woman Colby married. He wants me to continue to inspire. He wants me to continue to be kind. He wants me to continue to be respectful. He wants me to continue to be grateful. He wants me to continue to be the person he fell in love with. So that is my mission. It is who I am, and what I will continue to do. I feel I can do the impossible because I have been through the unimaginable

I still believe in miracles. It is the only reason, I can explain why I'm still here. A miracle. Over these last few years, I have learnt and come to believe that God has chosen something bigger for me than I could have ever imagined.

When Colb first died it took all that I had in me to keep my head above the water. I'd burst into tears at any given moment and the triggers were everywhere I looked. I constantly felt like I was drowning. In the first year of widowhood, I just did what I had to do to survive another day. In year 2, the shock slowly wore off and I got the chance to truly "find myself." The best way that I can explain it is I felt like I was a baby who just learned how to walk but at the same time, I was expected to run. And run fast. Although I couldn't run right away, I began to jog. Some days I was even able to outrun the waves or better yet, ride the waves. Some days I cry. Most days I laugh. Some days I take an "Em Day." But no matter what the days look like, I am reminded of how precious life is and how I don't ever want to take even one breath for granted. Today, I can honestly say I'm so glad I get to be here. And that feels really good to say.

So here I am, heading into year 3. Though I'm so far from having it all together. Though I still wonder why Colb had to be taken from me. Though I don't have all the answers for anyone that's going through what I went through. I know that I'm here. That I'm resilient. That I'm strong. Despite what the haters may say, I'm kind of a badass. I mean, I jumped out of a perfectly good plane to skydive with Colby's Uncle Riley in honor of our third wedding anniversary. I do many things, big and small for him now. I live life to the fullest. Colb is so dang proud of me. I used to always say, "One day closer to seeing you in Heaven, babe." To be honest, it is the only thing that kept me alive most days. It's still true. We are all one day closer to seeing the people that we've lost. I still can't wait to see him again. But not yet. My job is not done here. For now, I'm continuing to strive every single day to be his "little world changer."

"No one can teach you anything about healing, that you are not already going to discover for yourself. But other people can let you see that they made it through the same kind of pain, the same kind of heartbreak, the same kind of trauma. Other people can teach you how to be there for the person walking behind you."   - Unknown

For a long time, I felt the farthest thing from "graced" for this life. The word "Grace" was such a huge part of our marriage. It was a part of our everyday lives and how we strived to approach every situation that came our way.

"May we love beyond what the world understands and offer grace beyond what anyone could expect."   - Unknown.

That word was so important to us. I can't pinpoint the exact day, but it hit me, I felt graced for this life and my future, even when I didn't see it or feel it. I started looking back and seeing that God was slowly changing me so I could handle the things He was walking me through. It was then I started to have the courage to pray for my future, accept hard things, and remind myself it's God's will, not mine. Is it easy to accept this on hard days? No. Does this belittle the loss of Colb or trauma? Heck no. But it does give hope, sometimes lots, sometimes a little but there is a flicker of hope that's always in me now.

So, as I finish up this book, chapter 26, his first NHL number, and both our birthdays, I remind myself that I AM GRACED FOR THIS. And I'm telling you, that you are too. No matter what my future holds and no matter what the future looks like for you, WE are graced for this. Because God's grace runs deep in every season of our lives. It runs deep in our highs and our lows. Friend, if there is anything in the world that you can take from our story, it's that YOU can do anything. No matter the circumstances and no matter what obstacles you're faced with today, YOU are graced for this.

"You walked into the fire with him until the very end. You carry the torch of his legacy. There would be no memorial fund without you. There would be no book without you. You are his little world changer, Em. That's true love. That's Agape love. - Close Friend

Epilogue

"Joy and grief can coexist. I can be hopeful about the future and also feel sad about the past. I can be happy, and things still feel heavy. Life isn't one or the other; the presence of both signifies a full life."
- 2 Corinthians 4:18

As I said at the beginning of this book, I will never understand why I had to lose Colb. I look forward to the day when I get to Heaven and my life journey is explained to me.

I wanted to make sure I addressed my fellow widows as this book comes to an end.

One of the most common questions since losing Colb is how this has impacted my faith or the way that I look at grief now. What I have learned is that life will never be the same after experiencing a loss like this. There is such a stigma in today's society about grief. I had no idea part of my life's work would be trying to normalize grief for others who are struggling. However, I was left with this platform, and I have to use it. I have to trust that I'm strong enough to handle the pain that is necessary to process the normalizing of grief for others. On the days when pain comes, there will always be two of me. There is the me that is in agony and afraid, and then there is the curious one and at peace. The second me remembers that even though I can't know what will come next in my life, I know it matters. I will continue to remind others of this, and I hope this book did the same in helping normalize your waves that come with grief.

Here is the thing, I will always talk about Colb. Not because I want to live in constant pain but because this is my new world. I'd rather live honestly and out loud. Joy, love, happiness, and gratefulness are a part of my everyday life. But so is death, loss, heartache, and grief. I get giddy and excited about seeing Colb again in Heaven, but until then, I want to make him proud down here. So, I try to soak up every moment and try as hard as I can to spread every ounce of love I have to give. So, on that day, when I get to see him in Heaven I can run into his arms and tell him everything I was able to do. Not for me but because of him.

You see, God doesn't necessarily take our broken pieces and put them all back together, sometimes he adds new pieces. He helps us to rebuild while rebuilding us in the process. But that doesn't take away the past. I have learned through my grief, that no matter how painful, ugly, and broken I feel, my life can still be beautiful and full of love. I learned I can be hopeful for the future and even excited about it. There is new life on the other side of the unexpected, a life you never imagined. I feel like a hypocrite for saying this because I know how hard it was for me to hear and see this during my really hard moments. But I promise you, I see your pain because I have touched sorrow like you have and the intensity will not last forever. I know you never wanted to be a part of this club. I never imagined I would be a widow at the age of 26 but for whatever reason, I became one and because of that I see widows in a whole new light. I have felt the way society lacks understanding of grief and how damaging it can be. We all know death and loss are a part of life but until you're in it, you have no idea of the expectations and judgments that can come from others while grieving. I'm just here to tell you there is no blueprint for grief. There is no timeline.

Because the truth is, you will forever grieve the person you love. It is the price for loving.

A day will come, it may be sooner than you think, or it may be far away, and you may not be able to pinpoint the exact moment, but you will realize you were not made to suffer your whole life. It is not why you are here. YOU were made for more. There is still light inside you even when it feels completely extinguished. I see you. I see your pain. I understand this is a club that none of us asked to join. I can't teach you how to heal. I wish I could. But I hope my story will show you there are other people who have experienced the kind of pain you're experiencing. Other people are walking beside you and holding a space for you in their hearts. My hope for you is one day, you too will be able to look back and inspire others who are walking behind you on a similar, broken but beautiful journey. But until then, Heaven is cheering you on and so am I (and Chester too!)

Acknowledgements

"Thank you" will never do justice. There are so many people that have helped get me to where I am today.

First and foremost, MY FAMILY. The unsung heroes in this story. You have been there for me every second of this journey. You have picked me up from rock bottom. I would not be here today without you. You guys deserve your own book! I love you guys.

CHESTER. To my best bud. My furry little sidekick. The true MVP of this book. You got me out of bed every single morning. You were my reason to continue to live for so long. You gave me a purpose. You deserve all the treats and toys you want because you're the most perfect boy. (His vet even calls him perfect!) Forever. And ever. And ever.

MY THERAPIST. You have been with me since the beginning. Through the highs and the lows, you have supported me. You have taught me how to live again despite the pain. To have hope when I had none left. You have changed my life.

COLB'S BILLET FAMILY. From the moment I called to tell you of Colb's death, you have kept your promise to "get through this together." Thank you for always being there for me. Thank you for being family. Thank you for loving me so well for Colb.

CLOSE FRIENDS/HOCKEY COMMUNITY. Whether we are friends from hockey or outside of hockey, you are my people. I am so grateful for you all. You have rallied around me and honored Colb so well. I wish I could list you all, but you know who you are.

WIDOW(ER) COMMUNITY. I wish we were not a part of this club, but I am so thankful to have you all. You are often my first texts and calls. You get it like no one else. I have a feeling our people are up in Heaven so proud of us all and they're supporting each other too. Heaven is going to be one big party!

BRANDON AND TIM. There would be no book without you both. You made this dream come true. It is because of you this book is in so many hands all over the world. Thank you for helping me continue Colb's legacy.

COLIN AND THE BOIT FAMILY. You guys have been the greatest (unexpected) blessing. Your love and support have meant more than you will ever know. I feel so lucky to be a part of your family.

TO MY FOLLOWERS. I do not say this lightly, but you have saved me in so many ways. Your messages, comments, and continued support have reminded me that I am not alone in my darkest times. I can't reply to every message, but I read every single one. Thank you. Thank you for loving me. Thank you for loving Colb. Thank you for loving Chester. Thank you for now loving Colin too.

34595576R00114